To Ray

Hope you enjoy reading these stories

Love,
Mom and Bob

Y0-CBY-038

I DO

—◦◦◦—

MEMOIRS OF
MARRIAGE

Edited by Gisele P. Wolf-Klein, MD and Barbara Vogel, LMSW

TABLE OF CONTENTS

Introduction: *Falling in Love*   1

Chapter I: Marion and Norman: 66 years
                   The Single Marriage- So Last Century   5

Chapter II: Bob and Marge: 66 years
                   Part I. Marriage Vows   20
                   Part II: Living Through Our Marriage   23

Chapter III: Gladys and Morton: 61 years
                   The Fateful Day   31

Chapter IV: Marvin and Elise: 61 years
                   Forever and a Day   47

Chapter V: Rhona and Desmond: 59 years
                   From Guyana to Tennessee   58

Chapter VI: Sallie and Sherwood: 56 years
                   It was a Hot Saturday Night in July...   68

Chapter VII: Harvey and Phyllis: 55 years
                   55 Years and Growing   76

Chapter VIII: Grace and Leonard: 54 years
                   Love Letters and Much More   90

Chapter IX: David and Isabel: 54 years
                   From the Old World and the New
                   (and Everywhere in Between)   120

Chapter X: Terry and Cal: 51 years
                   The Fusion of Reality and Dreams   143

Chapter XI: Robert and Cinde: (51 years)
                   ...and Lilliana (13 years)
                   "For Twice in My Life"   161

Conclusion: The Last Word   190

Acknowledgments   193

INTRODUCTION

Falling In Love

On December 26, 1972, at 2:34PM, I fell. You might wonder, of course, how and why I would remember the exact time of a fall, so long ago? Well, you see, we, ski-instructors, belong to a professional class of highly trained super-heroes that never fall, and certainly never, ever, in front of our admiring clients. So, when after 34 minutes of agonizingly slow progress, multiple missed turns and ski-bindings openings, my 2PM client of the day fell again in deep powder snow and asked me to help him up, I promptly obliged him, counting the minutes until I would get rid of him for good. He was a brand new client, obviously a novice, flown over to the Swiss Alps for a pre-paid package ski tour from the USA. And I was part of the package, the "one hour lesson included with a Swiss ski instructor" before the traditional evening of raclette cheese and yodeling! Another 26 minutes, and I would happily rejoin my colleagues for a cup of hot chocolate and share stories of the day. And then, it happened: I reached out for his arm, solidly planted on my skis. He pulled me suddenly, purposely, causing me to lose my balance and laughing as I fell next to him on the gentle powder. While I was trying to regain control, he pulled my sunglasses off, looked into my eyes, and smiled. Here I was, sitting on the snow of my beloved mountains, next to a total stranger, who couldn't even ski. And it happened again: I fell one more time, at 2:35PM. This time, and for the first time of my life, I fell in love.

Falling in love was a rather complicated move for me, far more dangerous than a sharp turn on an icy slope in the invigorating early morning cold. For one thing, I was engaged to a very nice young student eager to start a family and get a golden retriever. I was also just starting my medical school, facing another four years of grueling classes, and a three years residency program in Europe. The immediate crisis was that I had no fancy clothes to wear for dinner at his hotel that night. So I declined his invitation and got him safely down the slopes. With palpable relief, and quite a bit of confusion, I took leave of him and greeted my three o'clock client. The snow was beautiful, warmed and softened by the afternoon sun. It was easy skiing and a well-known terrain, very reassuring. At 5PM, I joined all the ski instructors at the ski house for the mandatory daily report. At 6PM, I walked the two miles home, carrying my skis which had never felt so light. As I passed in front of the hotel where he had told me he was staying, I decided on the spur of the moment to walk in. He was playing the piano. He got up, smiled again and said "You came…" That night, I called my boy-friend back in the valley, and told him that I could no longer see him because I had just fallen in love with a man I had met three hours ago, a man who lived on the other side of the Atlantic Ocean, and who was returning to the USA in two days.

Four years later, we were married. I started my medical residency in New York in July 1976. At that time, there was only one Geriatric Medicine fellowship training program in the United States. It was located on Long Island, New York, and directed by the national leaders in Geriatrics, Dr. Leslie Libow and Dr. Felix Silverstone. I always knew I wanted to become a geriatrician, having had the privilege of being raised by wonderful, loving parents and extraordinary grand-parents. The stories they would share, their survival through two wars, their adjustment to modern technology never ceased to amaze me. As I learned the medical approaches to relieve some of the ailments which afflicted them, I would discover the joy of caring for them, and come to accept my inabilities to cure them of their infirmities.

As time passed and my clinical experience grew, I have had the privilege of caring for thousands of elderly people. I have also been blessed with the good fortune of working with a team of outstanding colleagues, nurses, social workers, physical and occupational therapists, secretaries. We have shared happy and sad moments together, raised our children, buried our parents, gone on diets, binged on chocolates, cried and laughed, fought and hugged. Together we have followed these elderly couples, our patients for over twenty years, reaching Shakespeare' sixth and seventh age:

> "The sixth age shifts
> Into the lean and slipper'd pantaloon,
> With spectacles on nose, and pouch on side,
> His youthful hose well sav'd, a world too wide,
> For his shrunk shank, and his big manly voice,
> Turning again towards childish treble, pipes
> And whistles in his sound. Last scene of all,
> That ends this strange eventful history,
> Is second childishness and mere oblivion,
> Sans teeth, sans eyes, sans taste, sans everything."

One recent winter, while skiing on the same mountains of my youth with my husband, with our two children and with their significant others, I finally realized that love can be truly eternal, no different in its strength, in its depth at 20 or at 80 or 90 years of age. I thought of all the couples I would see in my office, those bodies and faces wrinkled, arthritic and feeble. The expression in their eyes as they looked at each other, knowing with deep faith and total conviction that they would be there for each other until death do them part, despite whatever the doctor was about to tell them, whatever the results of the blood tests or the biopsy would reveal, that expression was indeed true love.

Upon returning from vacation, I shared my thoughts with Barbara Vogel the clinic social worker. She had counseled so many of these patients, she knew their life stories, their sorrows and their joys. Barbara, with her usual energy, optimism and humor, jumped at the opportunity to add one more project in our overwhelming clinical routine. We would ask couples to share their secrets for long term commitments through life. If enough of them would consent, we would then gather their stories into a book, where lovers of all ages could find guidance and support as they too walked the path of life.

There were only two criteria for selecting our contributors: they had to be married for at least fifty years to the same partner and they had to be experienced writers. Some of them had met in Guyana, some lived in India, some courted in the UK, in Portugal or in Nigeria. Some were physicians, some engineers, some home economists, some school teachers, some poets. But all of them, regardless of race, religion and socio-economic background, all of them have one essential thing in common.

All are in love.

In the following chapters, you will discover spouses struggling with unrealistic expectations, demanding in-laws, disruptive job transfers, financial woes, difficult children, illnesses and death. Real life. Tough, common problems. You will also encounter extraordinary individuals, blessed with the unique gift of true love, determined to constantly prioritize their spouse's well-being and happiness over any other need.

I know you will enjoy their company as you read their stories. You will laugh, you will cry, and you will cheer! You will become a better partner to your significant other as you learn, like they have, to truly appreciate life and love.

Gisele P. Wolf-Klein, M.D., New-York, September 2014

CHAPTER I:

Marion and Norman (66 years)

"The Single Marriage—So Last Century"
By Marion Gladney-Glasserow

There was still somewhat of a post war housing shortage in 1948. My soon-to-be husband and I were even shorter on available cash and steady income. To my father's great chagrin, his only daughter was planning to marry an unemployed disc jockey, in those days known more dignified as radio announcer.

After our quite elegant wedding atop the Hotel Pierre, we had originally planned to work and live in Washington, DC. But as Norman suddenly quit his job at WWDC Radio, we needed to retrieve the pots, linens and gadgets I had provisionally shipped to the two-room address we had rented in advance of the September wedding. My brother Ric was sent along as chaperone in my battleship gray Frazer. It soon developed a radiator leak requiring frequent stops for refills in the August heat. When we finally got to the apartment in which the three of us were planning to crash, the blast of DC summer that hit us when we opened the door sent us clear across the street to Hotel Statler's sumptuous air-conditioned luxury. We decided we could splurge for one night, all three bunking in one room.

With not one job between us, there was no time for a honeymoon and no money either. And with no place to live it was urgent to return and milk our contacts. Norman had sold his car so he could buy the traditional flowers for the wedding. I got us one winter's worth of a sublease in the building where my folks lived. But there were six weeks between the wedding and the apartment's availability. Where to? As luck would have it, Domestic Relations Court Judge and Mrs. Dunham of Riverdale firmly believed a house should not stand empty when there were needy kids like us and well to do folks like them who happened to travel a lot. We answered an ad and were shown a lovely home and garden by their son. When Norman finally got up the courage to ask "how much?" in a tone that strongly suggested, "we can't afford it anyway", the answer was "how is $35 a month, if it doesn't hurt you too much?" We arrived there after a 24-hour honeymoon in New York. There were fresh flowers in every room, a stocked pantry and refrigerator and a charming note from lady Dunham welcoming us into her home, and advising us that we were free to use any room, linens, dishes and even the golden harp in the formal dining room. Adam and Eve in paradise—fully equipped, including the apple tree in the garden. When I brought my Adam a lovely autumn apple, he said emphatically, "you can't eat that!" I am convinced the boy from Brooklyn thought only store bought fruit is fit for human consumption. But, I too, was not accustomed to suburban life. The Health Department stopped by one morning to ask if I had seen any evidence of rats. I blushingly said "no", since I quickly realized the bits of stale bread I had frugally left on the back stoop for the birds, I thought, had brought the local rat population to the attention of the neighborhood.

This was not the only beastly encounter in Eden. *The bride began to itch!* Too late in the summer for mosquitoes, wasn't it? When I showed off my welts and said I was sure they were fleabites, he pooh-poohed it, of course. "I can prove it to you". My father, a WWI vet, had told us that if you suspect fleas, fill a tub with water, remove your clothes *very slowly*, and shake them gently over the water. The fleas will jump in and drown. I performed! I had previous encounters with fleas when I lived in Brazil; but there I did the striptease without such an enthusiastic audience. Fleas in Eden probably left there by previous renters who took the dog with them but left the fleas behind. We could hardly afford an exterminator's visit for a ten-room house we didn't own. To call young Mr. Dunham was our only option. To soften what might be taken as an affront by this fine gentleman, Norman assured him of this unfortunate situation by saying, "My wife has had experience in this matter, sir." Ah! The bride from the slums, with upscale aspirations! One flea is preserved for posterity under scotch tape in our wedding album.

We never met the Domestic Relations Judge himself, but perhaps we inhaled some of his egalitarian wisdom while sleeping in his bed. Somehow we have managed six decades of jumping over marital hurdles. Of course, we stepped on each other's toes but also found ways of tiptoeing around our idiosyncrasies. Too often hurt feelings come from *unspoken* words. Not just the unnoticed vase of azaleas from the garden, the overlooked bandaged hand. No, the words WE supply, mentally, that he might say, should say, doesn't say, had better not say! We fill in the blanks. Library shelves are stocked with remedies which all boil down to "let it go". Easier said than done... What we lose when we lose our temper is the blood supply to the brain, "I was absolutely livid!" Yes, ashen, not red in the face. Winning isn't everything; it's the only thing…to avoid caring about. Norman is much better at that than I, thank goodness. What's my excuse? Growing up caught between two brilliant brothers is a powerful incentive for little Sis to strut her stuff whenever possible.

Throughout these sixty-plus years, we have pretty much each held up our own part of the sky, the necessities of living about which we had an unspoken division. If not, it's half-hearted and unsatisfactory to both. To avoid the blame game, it's great if everyone does what needs doing, avoiding the false hope "someone" will do it in your place. Experience ultimately proves that where you expect to find "someone" you generally find "no one". Sure, there were slip-ups. One balmy summer evening, sitting in our garden, we were surprised by a visit from the police with our youngest in tow. We had each been confident the other had put her to bed. "No one" had, and she decided to take an evening stroll in the neighborhood.

"They're writing songs of love"…but not about married life. That's not surprising. Marriage is not so much a ballad as it is a four act play. A time for hot romance and learning about each other… Years dedicated to nest making, career building and child rearing. The family matures and learns to withstand loss and manage gains and success with equanimity. Act four is said to be about "The Best Years". Then we will finally have time to…well, yes, maybe. My grandfather said, while turning his wedding band 'round and 'round, "Strange thing about a gold ring, the thinner it wears the heavier it gets."

Married life is a play in rehearsal – repetition, as the French say. That is what we do, repeat, re-hear, over and over. Mistakes and lessons learned, problems and solutions, promises and regrets, lies and atonement, victories and defeats… We are amateurs at a game no one teaches. There is no script. We ad lib, improvise, invent as we go along. At dawn we imagine the day; at night we write a critique. The most challenging scene is the finale, for then there is no curtain call, no reprise, no "Deus ex Machina" to reprieve the heroes.

Twenty years of school may be educational, but the curriculum does not offer "Family Finance", "Feud Facilitation", "Parent/Child Comprehension" and a whole catalog of other mysteries and complications that we try to learn on the job. And that includes sex- where the learning curve is fraught with bumps and detours, while media and entertainment pile on ideals that mostly defy reality.

Our marriage is purely an invention. We are as much alike as we are different. He eats his corn on the cob across, I eat mine in circles. We each came equipped with plenty of baggage, but also a talent for lightening the other's load. Most of all, we both have a strong sense of obligation, to each other, to our families, our heritage.

After the first phone call from this stranger I walked into the living room where my parents were entertaining and said, in slightly besotted tones, "I just heard the most *amazing* voice!" Norman had wisely used his sonorous radio host tones to get this girl's full attention. The tomboy in me suggested an ice skating outing for our first date; but that was not to be. I did not know then that the polio epidemic of 1940 had caught up with him, at 18, at summer camp and devastated his right leg and buttock with atrophy. We arranged for me to pick him up and drive to Greenwich Village for a drink at the Salle de Champagne. When I pulled up in front of the Riverside Drive apartment, waiting for me was this handsome Brooklyn-born sophisticate who leans into my window and says: "Hi, my folks are out. Would you like to come up?" My consciousness had not yet been raised and Woodstock was still a long way off. Things could only go up hill from there. (Maybe!... Some months later when the ring was offered it didn't fit; it was still the right size for the girl who had owned it, temporarily, before me.) Champagne loosened things up a bit. We talked about NYU, my alma mater, which he had also attended for a time. It was his professor there who had suggested he use the name Gladney for his radio career. Less Jewish than Glasserow... It stuck! And Gladney entertained me with uncanny imitations of Mayor La Guardia and FDR, but even more impressively, with inspired piano playing on the little upright at the bar. To this day, I am usually rewarded with a private piano recital while I am in the kitchen making dinner.

Norman was working in DC and I was a lowly secretary at Mutual Broadcasting in NY. We got to know each other through almost daily letters and occasional phone calls. When I became seriously ill, surgery left me forever unable to conceive. So now we were both damaged goods. I wasn't sure why we should bother to be formally wed since there would be no children. But he was determined to fix that. Soon after the wedding, our first appointment with the Stephen Weiss Adoption Agency was almost funny. We were such an unseasoned couple that I think they felt like giving us the lollipops. Several more interviews including an analyst's estimate of our parenting potential followed.

Some months later we received an official letter...of regret. The rejection turned me into a puddle of despair and him to adrenaline-fueled determination. "Now I know how to fight back" he said, and did, and won! I never found out how he did it, but eventually the call came; apparently there was a baby boy.

At a preliminary meeting the social worker said: "Before giving you some details, let me tell you that we always give the babies a temporary crib name; we call this baby Jeffrey." We looked at each other; "No need to tell us more, that _is_ the name we had chosen." I was thinking back to before I met Norman of the palmist I had gone to see, Margaret Mamlok, guru to Hollywood stars. She had *seen* that I would probably marry the fellow I was about to meet, and although she could not *see* children of my own, she found lines and swirls that indicated a powerful impact of children in my future. That was the year _before_ I became ill!

We were renters in our own apartment now in the same building as my parents. Two spacious rooms and a fold away kitchen. The new baby was, until legally adopted, still a foster child for several months. The law required visits from social workers and the child must have a room of his own. That meant giving up our bedroom to Master Jeff.

Wasn't it lucky that we had twin beds! My German upbringing had never included double beds; I considered them too proletarian. We stored the headboards and frames, bought eight short legs for the bottom of the box springs and created two couches, kitty-cornered in the living room. Home sewn covers and the bedding zipped into colorful pillows during the day— my first success at interior decorating. Over the years, I think we probably agree that one bed per person eases marriage past the more trying days, those you want to turn your back on. But beyond that it gives connubial visits, traversing the two-inch wide canyon between the mattresses, the aspect of an invitation, newness, romance, even conquest.

We were a traditional one-income family at the transitional mid-point of the century. We were able to afford household help, overseas vacations and a three-room garden apartment in Tarrytown, overlooking the Hudson. Norm's new executive position at the Bulova Watch Company, as director of advertising, included business trips around the country. Thus, pseudo-named N. Gladney hears about Edna Gladney, the mother-of-all-unexpected infants, founder of the adoption agency in Fort Worth, made famous by the movie, "Blossoms in the Dust". A fellow passenger was struck by the odd coincidence of the name, as the two dads were bragging about their kids on a flight to Texas. I had seen that film in my teens and remember still sobbing during the second feature film, a comedy.

How could we possibly fail on the providential path to expanding the family? Applications, appointments, months of waiting, planning, hoping and introducing three-year-old Jeff to the idea of sharing us with a sister. He apparently gave this a lot of thought. Daddy's wonderfully imaginative bedtime stories often included the specialness of "the chosen baby." But one day he decided to throw this question at me: "Why didn't she keep me?" While I hemmed and hawed, looking for age-appropriate wording, he gives himself the best possible answer; "I guess she just wasn't ready to have a baby at the time."

Aunt Edna, as the great lady was called by everyone, phoned on Mothers' Day in '54 to invite us to meet our daughter. Our beautiful baby-girl neither cried nor wet her diaper all the way home on the plane. We were so worried she might have a problem that I took her to the pediatrician right away to check her over, especially her vocal cords. He pinched her. She cried. We called her Liza Alison, in honor of the lead character, Liza Elliot in my cousin, Kurt Weill's Broadway musical, "Lady in the Dark".

Both of us were raised by parents who had gone through the First World War, the Great Depression, out-of-control inflation and WWII- on both sides of the Atlantic. That may have a lot to do with who we are and what we expect in life. We may be a bit less demanding and enjoy doing for ourselves. Waste is anathema to me; my Dad had us slit open empty envelopes to use as note paper. In war the motto was "Make it do; do it over, or do without". Frugality *is not* the F word!

When my trousseau was under discussion, a Persian lamb fur coat was generously offered –IF, as my Father put it: "You're sure it won't depress you to see it hanging in the closet because you have no place to go but the grocery store". Neither of us covets only the newest, latest, state-of-the-art, top-of-the-line. We live in the same house for over a half century. It's home, not a real estate investment. Memories echo in the walls. The ever-changing garden remembers the bar mitzvah, a confirmation, two weddings, and every birthday party. The furniture doesn't need updating since much of it is inherited antiques. Even the afore-mentioned horsehair mattresses are still as good as this union. Come to think of it, that either speaks well for their quality or it says more about our sex life than intended.

The Roaring Twenties when Europe freed the young from the fetters of the Victorians, my parents met, lived and loved till the end. That underlies my own understanding and approach to married life. I know it can be a minefield at times. If you don't want it to blow up you had better learn how to negotiate around the flash points.

Mother taught me early on: "IT" is bound to happen; human nature trumps common sense. Betrayal is in the LIES, not the act. Just make darn sure that SHE knows that you know all about it. That holds a mirror up to it, which takes the thrill out of it. It will become an incident, not an affair.

Only once did I go to Mother with a 'poor me' tale of woe. She basically said, "You made your bed, now lie in it." Harsh perhaps; but what good can come from rehashing every imperfection. Learn to make your own repairs. Foodstuff exposed to the air too long will spoil; so it is with "family stuff". Much of what passes through 'friended' eyes is downright pathetic, frequently dangerous. Down load the lowdown? To what end? Face to face is quite different from Facebook. It is possible to talk marriage to death. "Eighty percent of therapists practice marriage counseling, with poor results." Even Italy has a Divorce Fair; booths for free advice! Get to meet the mediator of your choice— not far from the Pope's throne.

In my supermarket you can get a free "Divorce Magazine", 45 glossy pages of long, helpful articles and dozens of lawyer ads. For those who are working on their pre-nuptial contracts, science has now found the fidelity gene; you can be tested to find out how you will handle commitment and temptation. Lots of luck! A German word for happy, merry, jolly is "fidel", it rhymes with female.

I have this small stack of business cards, each from a different company listing Norman as executive, account man, director of public relations, vice president of advertising, general sales manager, director of marketing. Several list him in the corporate name as partner or president. Each time it was an upward move. Once he was offered a partnership in a radio station in New Jersey. That time I dug in my heels. I felt the children should have the security of a hometown, a sense of belonging, something I had missed out on. Adoptive children may have a special need of such an anchor.

Before the end of the 50's we wanted to round out the family with one more adoption. The folks in Texas were more than willing. But this time we ran into an unseen reef that almost sank our ark. The sweet little bundle we brought home, a pink ten-day old girl, began day by day to turn darker. My mother knew to look for the Mongolian Spot, often visible at the base of the spine of non-Caucasian infants. The doctor confirmed it. The agency may not have known who the birth father was. Could we handle this? With two white kids in white suburbia? Would this be an additional burden for Liza and Jeff on being "different"? Race relations in this country were still abysmal in mid-century. It is remarkable how much the world has changed since then. We have no doubt we could handle it if it were now. But then we went through the hell of agonizing self-examination, doubt and, yes, feelings of shameful inadequacy. The Agency solved our and their problem when they brought us our beautiful Laura, this peaceful little golden girl, now mother of her own three wonderful young adults and wife to her recently retired U.S. Army colonel, whom she had met on a blind date at West Point.

After the sugar coated movies of the 40's and 50's come Consciousness Raising and The Pill. Now women are not merely educated, frustrated housewives, but they can aim for something other than nurse or teacher. Everything changes and with it marriage. Prime parenting time can start later or not at all. Dual career unions with different timetables, goals and opportunities for advancement—and adventure—may pull him and her to opposite coasts.

I was lucky. We had often worked together on Norm's projects. I wrote ad copy with my right hand while ironing or cooking with my left. When Laura reached high school age, the door opened for me to go back to work. An office, a desk and a secretary, YES! But his partners were not thrilled with the idea of a wife snooping around their office. Noticing things, such as extra-long 'interviews' behind closed doors, lunch hours that lasted until sun down. No doubt they feared their wives might want paying jobs, too. And how did my hero handle this dilemma? He reimbursed them my salary. Or, to put it another way, unbeknownst to me, I was paying myself. That was as close as we ever came to war. I quickly put a stop to that. And I stayed... And loved every minute of it. We drove to the city together each morning; did our dinner marketing in Queens on the way home. He helped a little in the kitchen; it was the best of times.

At first we worked mostly on ad campaigns. Then I took on the job of writing and producing a daily radio commentary for the actress Helen Hayes. We syndicated these five-minute talks countrywide. The subjects addressed the concerns of mature listeners, encouraging them to make the most of their "Best Years", the senior citizens whom I called Maturians. Doubleday published many of these essays in expanded version in two books. There was much to choose from; we broadcast 5 days a week for 5 years. Perhaps "The First Lady of the American Theater" recited more of my prose than the Bard's—volume, not quality, to be sure.

Parenting is playing at being a deity. But we are not gods and we cannot create in our own image. Is it easier with adoption? Yes, in some ways. At least we know they don't "take after" anyone in the family. And, yet, we think we can control who they will be. NOT! Family life is the ultimate soap opera. Eventually everything that could happen does. Military school, was that the right thing for him? The college of her choice, on the other side of the country? A first marriage, so young! More than one divorce... Living too near; moving too far away. Abortions and conversions—one out of our religion, one into it

You learn to ride it all out. Until lightning strikes...twice! Liza died of a cerebral aneurism in 2001, at the age of 47. Four years later, Jeff at 55, crashed his light plane in a New Jersey field. I can write these two-dozen words now— on one quick breath, like a run- on sentence. But I still can't say them. It's not supposed to happen. But it does, to too many parents, everywhere, everyday, for no apparent reason. Somehow you learn to live with it. And pretend not to know that the next upper cut to the jaw is already in the master plan.

You may have noticed that not much has been said in this recitation of long-playing wedded bliss about passion or sex. I leave it to poets and fiction writers who do it so much better than I can. In the final analysis, enduring love is rooted in respect, admiration, cooperation, individualism, freedom and common goals. And, yes, it does last a lifetime. Or so I am told, several times a day, by the one man in my life.

As the dutiful wife, I will give him the last word, a letter he wrote to my parents during our honeymoon. My father carried it in his wallet throughout his life. Our granddaughter describes the letter as "so last century":

"Dear Mother and Dad,

You might want to know something about us as this unique living together unfolds. There is a wonderful look in Marion's eyes. It was not expected that she, so soon, resolve the heartache of several months back. It's the result, most fortunately, of two people falling in love, living together in love – a tremendous feeling of peace and utter faith in each other and the future. Out of all the strain and obstacles encountered by both of us through our youth and into maturity, has come the strength to cope with anything. I did not intend to wax too sentimental. But when two people are completely happy, their good fortune should be shared. I must thank you for Marion as she is everything I ever read or dreamed, but never knew 'til now.

Your "third son", Norman."

THE SECRET TO MARION AND NORMAN'S MARRIAGE?

THE POWER OF MUSIC

"I just heard the most amazing voice" announced Marion to her bewildered parents, after she received a phone call from a total stranger. She was so taken with Norman's "sonorous radio host tones" that she agreed to meet with him.

On their first date, Norman decided to impress his new girlfriend with an "impromptu piano recital on the restaurant's little upright"*...Norman was such a charming pianist and singer... He had suffered from the 1940 polio epidemic which left him with severe leg atrophy, she was an enthusiastic ice-skater.*

Even though Marion's father, to say the least, was extremely reluctant to encourage her daughter's interest in an unemployed disc jockey, in those days known as a "radio announcer", she persisted and married Norman with the beautiful voice.

Music carried them both through the trials and tribulations of married life. When it became clear that Marion would not be able to conceive, they both decided to adopt a child. However, as they returned from the adoption agency with their brand new baby girl, they became alarmed when the newborn did not cry. They were so worried that they took her to the pediatrician right away to check her over, "especially her vocal cords". When she cried, they called her Liza Alison, in honor of the lead character of the Broadway musical "Lady in the Dark", written by Marion's cousin, composer Kurt Weill.

Have you ever noticed how a tune on the radio can bring us back to memories of events long gone? Old Broadway tunes, love songs, lyrics and rhymes melt us away in an instant. Musical imagery has been extensively studied: one can replay music by imagining it. On PET scans, the cerebral blood flow has been shown to increase with auditory imaging.

Music provokes emotions, both positive and negative which activate similar regions in the frontal brain regions, as can be demonstrated using EEG. Happy songs show increased activity in the left frontal part of the brain, while sad tunes create activity primarily in the right frontal part of the brain.

The tones in human speech, filled with emotions, are very much like the tones in music. The highly pleasurable experience of listening to music is often described as "giving the chills". A recent study from The Montreal Neurological Institute and Hospital at McGill, published in the journal Nature Neuroscience, describes that the mere anticipation of pleasurable music can induces dopamine release, as do food, drug, and sex. The authors, Blood and Zatorre used PET scan technology to measure changes in the cerebral blood flow of subjects listening to music that gave them the "chills" or "musical frisson", best described as a peak emotional response to music. An increase in cerebral blood flow was seen in several brain regions such as the amygdala, the orbitofrontal cortex, the ventral striatum and the midbrain, known to be more active during pleasant activities which result in positive emotion and arousal.

On the other hand, when unpleasant melodies are played, the PET scan shows activity in the posterior cingulate cortex which correlates with emotional pain and social rejection (Eisenberger).

Marion and Norman have shared 66 years of married life. It has not always been blissful. Two of their adopted children died as adults, one from a brain aneurysm, the other in a plane crash. A third adopted child was returned to the adoption agency because neither Marion nor Norman could face the realities of raising a bi-racial child in white suburbia in the 1950's. That child was replaced by another newborn, daughter Laura, "leaving them with feelings of shameful inadequacy"…And of course, like many wives, Marion had to face "IT ": It is bound to happen, human nature trumps common sense. Betrayal is in the LIES, not the act…" Through it all, they have continued to enjoy music, have learned to forget and forgive.

At the age of 91, Norman was still playing the piano as well as ever, though his brain had been devastated by Alzheimer's disease…

CHAPTER II

Bob and Marge (66 years)

"Marriage Vows & Living Through Our Marriage"
By Robert Schreibman

Part I. Marriage Vows (1937-1941)

A man and woman joined in wedlock for life.

The legal and intimate union of a man and a woman.

A couple formally declaring the vows of marriage *"To have and to hold, to love and cherish, for richer or poorer, in sickness and in health, until death us do part".*

Are these just words without meaning?

Does any thought accompanied these beautiful and profound words or are they merely superficial utterances that are just a small part of the marriage celebration?

The solemn procession, the vows, the ceremony, the music, the dancing, the festive dinner, are they all meant for naught?

My generation, I'm 95 years old, doesn't think so. We believe in the longevity of marriage and we have the credentials to prove it. Please listen and understand what we have to say. We each have our own unique life story to relate that we hope is interesting and thought provoking to you. By the way, that portion of the marriage vow, *"Until death us do part"* does not end there. For me, my deep feeling of love dictates, *"Until death us do part and then continues on to eternity."*

We, of the nonagenarians' generation, have life stories with a similar ring to it. We met our partner in life while in high school. We courted in our teens. Our first date. Our first kiss. Holding hands throughout a movie show. The walk home and usually a detour to the local ice cream parlor for refreshments.

The innocence of our relationship and the slow, rich development to our maturity added to the richness of our beginning. Then, World War Two came along and interrupted any plans we had for our immediate future. But I'm getting ahead of myself. So hear my story. Our story. The story of Marge and Bob.

We were young, we were carefree and we were happy. It was the year 1937. October. High School graduation was three months away. What a wonderful time in our lives... We were so innocent of the distant war clouds that were gathering over Europe and Asia. Marge would be 16 in December and I just turned 17. Halloween was coming up and my friends and I were invited to a Halloween party. I made it known I wouldn't attend as I had no date to accompany me. My friends insisted they would provide a blind date. After much persuasion, I finally agreed.

Well I hit the jackpot! There was this beauty being introduced to me. Marge was her name and our love affair lasted 70 years, 66 years of it in marriage. How's that for a blind date? The introduction was quite simple. I said, "Hello, I'm Bob." She said "Hello, I'm Marge." There you have it. Thus, the beginning. It was something special. It had to be. Little did we realize that at that moment was born a whole lifetime of wonderful memories that I can conjure up at any time, as a projector shining on a screen, and be able to visualize each treasured moment.

At the beginning, it wasn't a whirlwind courtship. After the party, I walked her home. We lived in the same Bronx, New York neighborhood. Saying goodnight at her door, I politely requested a good night kiss. We did that in those days. Politely asked. How times have changed. After a fashion, I was rewarded with my goodnight kiss and floated all the way home.

I was busy in my senior year at De Witt Clinton H.S., an all boys' school. Marge attended nearby Walton H.S., an all girls' school. We kept in touch by telephone. No cell phones in those days. Whenever my schedule allowed, I would try to intercept her on her way home from school and would proudly carry her books. I was really smitten. She was my girl and I felt good.

From the very beginning of our meeting and for the next four years we were an inseparable couple. Weekends were a joy. I remember it all. A Saturday night movie, a neighborhood dance, summer picnics, family get-togethers, band concerts in Bronx Poe Park, the annual City College Spring boat ride to Bear Mountain and the moonlight sail back to New York. Sundays were spent exploring and enjoying the sights of New York. Museums, Central Park, Broadway theaters and stage shows, and a multitude of famous restaurants to choose from. And friends, so many friends, all of us experiencing the youthful life together.

As we matured, serious thoughts of marriage became a popular topic. We were faced with a dilemma. The paramount question wasn't do we marry, but when. World War two was on the horizon and our generation had to deal with the draft into the armed forces and an unknown future. Do we marry before we are drafted or wait until we return? If we return! We were, by then, all so in love. Amongst our friends, it became an individual choice and monumental decision. Marge and I chose "before" and we prayed for our future.

August 20, 1941. It was a simple wedding. Just the immediate family and very close relatives. Nothing lavish in those days... It was a time of war and shortages were common. And to be honest, money was also in the shortage category. What was not in short supply were our wedding vows.

"To Have and to Hold"

"To Love and To Cherish"

Expressed with all its fervor and deep meaning and great resolve...

PART II. Living Through Our Marriage (1941- 2007)

There is no denying the uniting in marriage of two different personalities requires understanding, a shared respect, and compatibility. Surely, **to love and to cherish**, should overcome any bump in the road. That vow should grow in intensity and never, ever diminish.

Our first home was a furnished room with a shared bathroom in the hall. Our rent was $288 per year. No opulence there. We were still too young to have amassed any wealth or worldly possessions. My income, common in those days, was $21 per week. That's $1092 per year. I nitially, Marge worked in retail sales and earned much less. It was a very modest beginning. What did it matter, we were young and in love and we had a whole future before us.

"For Richer or Poorer"

Yes, *"for richer or poorer"*. We were experiencing, the *"for poorer"* segment. It didn't matter. We'll be patient while we awaited the arrival of the *"for richer"*. At the time, our monetary wealth consisted of our weekly income and a bank savings account of seventy- five dollars.

We moved into a one bedroom apartment where, 18 months later, February 23, 1943, we were blessed with a son. We eventually would have two great grandchildren. That's improving our wealth.

Twenty- three months into our marriage, July 9, 1943, I was called for the draft and served 2 and a half years. Sometime during the year 1944, I found myself with my army unit, in a staging area, waiting to go overseas at a New Orleans Port of Embarkation. An unusual and radical turn of events found us on a troop train, rather than an ocean liner, being shipped, we subsequently discovered, to a highly secretive location in Oak Ridge, Tennessee, known now as The Manhattan Project, the birthplace of the atomic bomb.

As a combat M.P. Unit, initially, our mission was to secure and fully protect the entire Manhattan Project area. Needless to say, we operated in very sensitive areas and secrecy was paramount. After several months, I and three others from the unit were given a special assignment at the Project which, given the nature of the assignment, resulted in no hope for any future furlough. With that in mind, Marjorie decided to come to Tennessee with our son. We rented an apartment in a nearby town, after I was given permission to live off base as a non-commissioned officer. With the world in a turmoil, we were blessed and so fortunate to be together once again as a family.

Knowing Marjorie, after a very short period of time, I could see her become restless and want to go to work and release her pent-up talents. So we made arrangements with a neighbor to daily baby-sit our son. Marjorie applied for and was hired immediately at the Manhattan Project pending government security clearance. After a short period of time, her security clearance was issued.

A marriage with no secrets between couples is a requisite for smooth sailing. Yet, here we both were facing a violation of that very fundamental rule. I knew her work required her to handle very sensitive papers and documents but nothing was ever discussed or revealed. It remained that way all our life. You would think, that just once, in the throes of heated sexual activity, there would have been a weakness and a letdown of the cloak of secrecy and the answer to my casual question, "So dear, what did you do at

Oak Ridge?" would be forthcoming. It never was answered. Well, it never was answered in a civilized way. That was the last of my unusual method of interrogation and the revelation of her very staunch characteristic.

But the story doesn't end there. After the war, Marjorie eventually was employed by Bulova Research and Development as assistant personnel manager. The R & D Division of Bulova was converting to U.S. Government contracts in the development of military weaponry and all personnel were required to possess government security clearance. Along with all the engineers, Marjorie filed for clearance. They all received the standard general security clearance. However Marjorie's papers came back with the highest top security issued by the U.S. Government. Obviously, a reflection of her wartime employment. At the time, General Omar Bradley was CEO at Bulova. He came to the building one day and requested to meet the "young lady" who possessed such top security. When she presented herself, he inquisitively asked her what DID she do at The Manhattan Project to warrant such unheard of top security. She just smiled and said, "General, you should know better than that". I could have told him even my unique interrogation technique got nowhere.

I was very proud of her impeccable integrity and proud to say I loved this wonderful woman and most of all, she loved me. And that made me feel good.

Well, we prevailed and I was discharged in April 1946, returning home to New York where our life together resumed, blissfully, despite the interruption. But all is well that ends well. We were still holding hands and very much in love and happy.

We prospered. Our son grew up and married and now we had a grandchild. A successful business life produced a comfortable retirement which allowed Marjorie and I to travel worldwide and enjoy our senior years. We enjoyed the sights throughout America just as we enjoyed the sights of New York together when we were single. We also traveled, at various times, throughout Europe, North Africa. Greece and the Greek

Islands. Israel, England and all of Italy. Always holding hands, enjoying one another, and being in love. By now, we experienced both ends of the spectrum. Our status now appeared to be, not wealthy, but a comfortable *"for richer"*.

For the most part, we enjoyed good health. A little setback here and there but generally we coped. I experienced triple bypass surgery. Marjorie had a very serious digestive problem that required several years to be finally corrected. We persevered.

Then suddenly our ecstasy was shattered. Life dealt us a terrible blow when, in September of 2000, after a few uncomfortable but revealing incidents, Marjorie was diagnosed with Alzheimer's.

The next eight years were devoted exclusively to Marjorie, providing for all her needs and comfort and contending with every conceivable weapon in the Alzheimer's arsenal.

Throughout it all, Marjorie remained at home. We would weather the storm together and I would be her sole caregiver.

As the disease progressed, she became calmer, more subdued, sweet, loving, and childlike. Despite the hardship, as a 24/7 caregiver, I loved taking care of her. It was truly a labor of love. And why not? After all, we were still, as always, very much in love. Remember our vows and their meaning?

"In sickness and in health"

Idle words? No, they are certainly not. So now we were testing our vows to the utmost once again, *"in sickness"*.

Sixty-six years ago we held hands, under God, and promised, in solemn vows, the truth of our feelings. Yes, *"In Sickness and in Health"*.

We met as a blind date in 1937 on Halloween. Seventy years later, on Halloween eve 2007, while eating dinner, Marjorie suffered a devastating stroke. Eleven days later November 10, 2007, under Hospice care in our home, she peacefully died in my arms as we held hands.

Once again our vows, for the last time, became very pronounced

"Till Death Us Do Part—-

Now I, with all sincerity and from deep within my heart and soul, added to the vow,

And Then, On to Eternity........forever"

We always believed in the longevity of marriage and the sanctity of our vows. Yes, we do have the credentials to prove it.

Among many youngsters of the present generation, we witness so many, many separations and divorces. Look around. Very few families escape the tragedy. It is sad that so many children's lives are disrupted and deprived of the warmth and richness of the family unity.

Our family didn't escape. Our son married and then divorced. His son, our grandson, floundering in confusion, questioning: "Why? Why? Why?..." And always with the secret hope that his parents will, some day, remarry and all will be right again. It never came to pass. It very rarely does.

In our family, we faulted neither of the principles. They are two love-able people. Our son is a good person and so was his wife, Kate. We love them both. The separation and ultimate divorce was very civilized and amicable and, to this day, shows no visible signs of hostility. For a short while, we too harbored our grandson's thought. Maybe they will remarry someday and all will be right again. It never came to pass. However it did become right in its own way. Our son found and married another very lovely woman. They will be celebrating their 25th wedding anniversary this year.

After the divorce, we remained " Mother and Dad" to our ex-daugh-ter-in-law, who lost her parents early on, and we maintained constant and current communication never losing sight of the close relationship and love fostered by Marjorie.

It culminated on November 14, 2007 in an unusually rare but beautiful and loving eulogy presented by an ex-daughter-in-law to an ex-mother-in-law. In the saddest moment of my life, listening to Kate's adulation, I, once again, felt so very proud of the woman I loved, in marriage, for 66 years.

Do I believe in love at first sight? No, I do not. I believe in attraction at first sight. Love is a slow development. Love takes time. Love has to grow from within, to be nourished and be allowed to blossom into full bloom. Couples should be patient with their differences and be tolerant of their likes and dislikes. Be respectful and proud of one another. Grow together, intellectually, and yes, sexually. Without these fundamentals, you are asking for trouble.

Would I do it again? Absolutely! After our first meeting in 1937, we courted for four years and married in 1941. We were married for 66 wonderful years.

If some spiritual power granted us the miracle privilege to relive our lives exactly the same, all over again, from the very beginning, I would start this very moment. Imagine being twice blessed enjoying a lifetime of happiness, sharing life all over again and in love with a most unusual and fascinating woman.

I'm alone now and I rely and depend heavily on wonderful memories to ease the pain.

So that's our story. The love and vows of Marge and Bob... It will live on through eternity. That is my vow.

THE SECRET TO ROBERT AND MARGE'S MARRIAGE?

THE POWER OF TOUCH

Barbara and I remember well one of the last visits we had with both Marge and Robert in my office. They were sitting together, across my desk, holding hands, as I was discussing Marge's medications regimen. She was quite advanced in her illness, unable to express herself, unable to comprehend my recommendations. He was sharing his attention between his beloved wife and the two of us, his professional team, trying to grasp all of my therapeutic suggestions, while keeping his eyes on her at all times.

Half way through the consultation, she became a little bit agitated: she had noticed a wrinkle on his jacket and wanted to smooth it out. He bent a bit to facilitate her reach, and the gesture became a caress…

They looked at each other and kept touching each other as they did when they first met, young teenagers in the Bronx. When they first met on a blind date, Halloween 1937, they "spent the entire evening holding hands". *She was calm now, she was smiling at him, and he was lost in her eyes…*

There has been impressive research demonstrating the power of touch in daily communication, whether it be in marital relationships, sports activities or business encounters. A high-five given by a favorite coach to a school athlete can lead to a win for the team. A gentle touch on the shoulder may reassure an anxious candidate during an interview.

In 2010, a study reported that "Good teams tended to have more touches than bad ones, with the league's top two teams—the Boston Celtics and the Los Angeles Lakers- being the most touch-bonded teams. At the same time, the least touchy teams- and the least successful- were the Sacramento Kings and Charlotte Bobcats"

The scientific basis for the power of touch is the release of oxytocin, a hormone which helps create a sensation of peace and trust, and decreases the stress hormone cortisol. The body responds to the release of oxytocin with a feeling of relaxation, which allows for mutual satisfaction.

Robert and Marge had discovered the power of touch. They used it every day, at every opportunity. They used it in their youth, enjoying their lives and shared intimacy, they used it as they aged and faced illnesses, they used it to soothe each other in the ultimate goodbye.

On Halloween night, seventy years later, she suffered a stroke at home and "died peacefully in my arms as we held hands".

CHAPTER III

Gladys and Morton (61 years)

"The Fateful Day"
By Gladys McConnell

September 3rd 1939. It was a beautiful Sunday morning as we were ending our holiday on the cliffs in Norfolk overlooking the North Sea. The sun was shining, there was a nip in the air and the sea was a sparkling blue – so tranquil and peaceful. But there was also a tension in the air as people were waiting for the speech from the Prime Minister. As they crouched over their radios the devastating announcement came over the air waves telling the English people that we were at war with Germany. Little did I know that this historic event would shape my life forever.

We did not know what to do. We did not know where to go. We did not know what to expect. There was fear that the skies over London would be blanketed by German war planes raining destruction over the city. But nothing happened. I was waiting to start College in London, but all the schools and Colleges evacuated to places farther afield for safety. It was decided that I should stay with friends in Cambridge until I knew where the College had gone. My brother and sister should join the thousands of school children who were sent out into the country, while my parents returned to London. Little did they realize that they would not see their younger children for five years as all unnecessary travel was prohibited.

We were all issued gas masks which became a permanent appendage wherever we went and we all had ration books. As I look back I do not know how anybody managed to survive on the meager amount of food we were allowed. Clothing was also rationed with coupons and if you had a new coat there were not enough coupons left for shoes or anything else for the year. We became adept at turning old curtains into skirts, blankets into warm coats and sheets into summer dresses. Brides were in ecstasy if they could manage to get an old parachute to make their wedding dress. It was a time that became a way of life, and it would last for many years after peace was declared. It was the era of make do and mend and make the best of what you have.

During College vacations I returned home to London to face night after night of air raids in the London Blitz, but that is another story, all stemming from that fateful day in Sept 1939.

Anglo-American Relations

London was a lonely place for young servicemen from abroad in the 1940s who had never been there before. I was doing volunteer work at an

American Officers Service Club and our job was to be information ency-clopedias for soldiers on leave. "Go and see if you can help that young man sitting by himself over there as he looks lost" I was told. I approached the young airman and introduced myself. He said his name was Bob McConnell and he was from Indiana and had never been to London before. We chatted about his home, his girlfriend that he had just got engaged to, and that he knew very few people over here.

I was on a week's holiday from teaching Home Economics. He asked me if I would go to the theatre with him that week as it was his birthday and he did not want to spend it alone. After a pleasant evening I invited him to visit our family for tea the next Sunday. Americans were not regarded as the most desirable of company they were considered "over paid, over fed, over sexed and over here" and my mother was horrified at the thought of "one of those" coming to tea. Bob duly arrived and in a short time the family was charmed by him. After that he regularly used to drop in when he was in London to visit with my parents. I was engaged to a dashing, handsome, romantic Spitfire pilot and did not realize at the time that he was selfish, undependable, unreliable and unpredictable - I was captivated.

After Bob returned to the States a few months later, he married and we all corresponded once in a while. The following year we had a let-ter from Bob to say that his younger brother, a bombardier on a B17, was being sent to England and asked if he could visit our family as Bob had done. My mother was delighted this time and looked forward to meeting the next McConnell and he arranged to visit the following evening. The weather was terrible – a thick inky black pea soup fog that enveloped one like a blanket, which choked your lungs and made visibility nonexistent. The bus stop was only two blocks away but nobody could see more than a few inches in front of them. I went out with my flashlight and waited for the buses. As everybody stepped off the bus I shone the light on them and asked if they were Morton McConnell. The fog was so thick that some of the buses went at walking pace led by one of the blind who did not need light. Finally a voice out of the darkness answered that he was Morton and

I led him home. Not having seen whom I had met off the bus we went indoors and I met Morton for the first time. He too, visited my parents during his stay in England and when he returned to the States we kept up an interesting correspondence. My romantic Spitfire pilot had broken our engagement and Morton was there offering great support. He was loving, kind, and very caring. I sometimes answered his letters, sometimes not. He thought he had the largest collection of English stamps in the war. After writing for three years Morton returned to England for a summer hoping that I would go back to America with him. I stayed in England. I did not want to leave my country or my close and loving family but the bricks of loyalty and love had built a foundation that was gradually turning into a feeling deeper than friendship. We looked at the world through different glasses and saw the same view. A warm, comforting relationship was building with a steady glow that overcame all obstacles. With the persistence of the McConnells, Morton continued to write for two more years when he wore down my resistance and I knew that life without Morton would not be complete. I sailed for NY where I have been ever since. Volunteering does have its rewards and shows up in strange ways

Back Home in Indiana

Morton was born in Indianapolis and grew up in southern Indiana with his three brothers. He was quiet and rather shy and tagged along with his older brother Bob. Morton was a child of the Depression and knew need and loss and want. Their father was the patriarch of the family and ruled with a rod of iron - he did not like British people and was not slow to show it. He reminded me of the King of Siam in "The King and I". His mother was a sweet gentle woman who adored her husband. She came from a Quaker family of only females and her father was manager of a Dog and Pony Circus that traveled the Far West so he was rarely home. It must have been a shock to her to produce four boys. They were a devoted family and the boys were taught to be creative and do everything around the house. Morton was sent to Purdue to study engineering even though his heart was not in it. Instead he became involved in all aspects of technical theatre work and finally transferred to the Goodman Theatre School in Chicago. Several years after his father died his mother married a wonderful widower who was a retired doctor from the South. Like a caterpillar turning into a radiant butterfly, Sybil emerged. Instead of wearing somber browns and grays she wore becoming pinks, romantic lavenders and dreamy blue colors. They had about 15 idyllic years together, traveled all over Europe, ate out at the best restaurants and the boys were delighted.

They'll Always be an England

I had been born and grew up in London with my younger sister and brother. My mother was the disciplinarian of the family and I adored my Dad. He took us all over London sightseeing every weekend to learn about all the historic sites. My mother had five sisters and for a time I was the only grandchild – I had a lovely childhood. We had little in the way of material things but made up for it in love.

We respected our parents and obeyed them. We worked for what we needed and appreciated it all the more. Nowadays it seems that children rule the family and parents provide all that is demanded. Many of the wives work these days. The children are channeled into so many planned activities that they do not have time to ride their bikes or play ball in the neighbors' backyard. There are no teen age babysitters, no boys to cut the grass or shovel snow and no local newspaper boy. There are TVs, computers and easy air travel. It makes it hard for young people to create a sense of togetherness as we had. Few people sit around the fire in the evening and listen to the radio together, write letters, knit, mend and discuss the day.

New York

Morton and I were married in Chicago in a frigid snowstorm in the beginning of January 1950. We stayed there until he graduated the following spring. Our wedding was a somber affair as there was only Morton's family and a few friends and all the McConnells arrived all dressed in black. I overheard his father say that it would never last ... Sorry Sir, it has only lasted 60 years and is still going strong!! Travel by plane was still nonexistent so we had to do with phone calls to include my family who were delighted.

After Morton's graduation we felt equipped to conquer the world. With two suitcases, $65 between us, and our hearts full of high hopes and great expectations we made our way to the big city whose streets were supposedly paved in gold. The next day we scanned the New York Times Want Ads and went our separate ways - Morton to find a job in the entertainment world, and I to find somebody who could use an English Home Economist. Footsore and weary at the end of the day we met back at our room. The following day we set off again and Morton hit the jackpot. CBS Television was looking for a Lighting Director. He was hired – a temporary job that lasted for 35 years. Soon after, CBS created a Special Effects Department which appealed to Morton greatly.

It was live. It was unpredictable. It was exciting. It was Television in the 1950's. Morton thought like Rube Goldberg – the originator of complicating simple tasks into giant and muddled complexity. So now we had a Special Effects Director who went to work and played all day.

It was the days of Edward R. Morrow– always a cigarette dangling from his lips and a brilliant newscaster. The days of stony faced Ed Sullivan who launched so many future stars.

Garry Moore, Captain Kangaroo, Comedians Danny Kaye, Red Skelton, singer Perry Como and a host of others who entertained us in those early days. These were Morton's playmates at work.

The Department was called upon to produce any and all Special Effects from snow laden trees in the heat of the summer, to explosions, fire and the rear projection of the nightly news graphics. But with live TV whenever the rest of the world was at home, evenings, weekends and holidays, was when the department had to work.

One day Morton was called upon to create a bubble bath for Zsa Zsa Gabor. Little did the audience know that Morton was standing at the other end of the tub blowing air into it with a vacuum cleaner. Tough day! Red Skelton demanded a toaster that would hurl a piece of toast into the air so that it landed in a certain spot. When they performed "For Whom the Bell Tolls", in the middle of a New York heat wave they had to haul in loads of snow and pack it on to the branches of the trees before it melted.

Another time they were filming a new red lipstick commercial for Revlon in an old New York loft – it took a long time and there were troughs of fire in front of the set. All of a sudden all the fire sprinklers started pouring water from the ceiling, alarm bells rang, the New York City Fire Department arrived in full force at the front door while Morton and his crew slipped out the back.

The Space shots were unforgettable, as they were still done live, keeping the staff at the studios for days at a time, snatching sleep whenever and wherever they could. Responsibility for the mockup of the moon walk kept the department very busy. One day the model moon rover on the got stuck in a crater. A large hand filled the screen and Walter Cronkite announced, "That's not the hand of God on the screen saving the Rover, it's the hand of Mort McConnell putting things in place on the moon. "

The long and irregular hours of Morton's schedule were very hard on the rest of the family. With four small boys and a house to look after and no help, support group or family, I often wonder how I survived. Unlike most people all the friends I grew up with, whom I went to school with, who knew my family were 3,000 miles away. I did not have a similar background and felt uprooted, transplanted in a dry and arid soil. Morton was a workaholic and was happy on his own. I liked people and needed them in my life. It was a very lonely living in a completely male oriented world with no female companionship and I had to find other outlets to meet people. I took up watercolor painting which led to a hobby of 45 years. I volunteered at the local hospital where I met many people and I got a part time job in a pediatrician's office and met lots of other Mothers. It was then that I learned that there is only one person you can rely on and that is yourself. It was a hard lesson to learn.

The tables were turned when taped shows came into practice. Who was this man that was now at home in the evenings and at weekends? Life became more normal and less hectic and was terrific.

Was it a job or was it play? All of the actors who were then unknown were just coworkers that met every day.

Time has passed their names down in history. Television nowadays is nothing like it used to be. Computers now create sophisticated images, sound has improved, screens have become larger but the old programs which still appear regularly cannot be beaten.

I had some challenging and interesting jobs in New York in the Home Economics field before our children were born. I worked as a food stylist, a food editor and later created some cookbooks for a hospital and church as a volunteer contribution. I loved my work and still try out and create new recipes each week for my family.

Vacation Break

By now we had found a house we liked in the suburbs of Long Island and had four sons. Life was busy. We had no help, no extended family and were really on our own. I could not have coped without the help of my better half. We had wonderful family holidays at Cape Cod – our favorite place in the world.

It was a long and hot journey to the Cape with the car piled to capacity with all the paraphernalia that we had to take, and four tired and sticky little boys. We reached the bridge that spans the Cape Cod Canal and as we crossed it a magical thing happened. All the tension, and worries dropped, as if into the canal below and a wonderful sense of peace and serenity descended on us. I don't know if it was the smell of the scrub pine, the soaring of the gulls in the fresh balmy air or the glimpses of the sparkling blue water beneath the expanse of clear blue sky as we sped along Route 6 to Eastham. We finally reached our cottage and the spell was cast.

Each year the magic of the Cape has lured us back – sometimes the cottages were little more than shacks, sometimes quite charming but it only took a couple of hours to make it our own. One year we found our dream house, nestled on a dune, overlooking the calm shallow beach on the bay. After that, we returned year after year.

People used to ask us what we did at the Cape. We didn't "do" anything – we just became part of the Cape and enjoyed every minute of it. The boys never lacked for things to do – they built castles of their dreams in the sand, dug for clams, searched for sea shells, flew their kites on windy days and paddled in the shallow pools left when the tide went out.

As the years went by we added four bicycles to the back of the car and perched a sunfish sailboat on top – no wonder people stared at us as we made our way along the thruway. There were old Indian walks to explore, long bicycle rides and the water there to sail the sunfish. And always at dusk the spectacular Technicolor sunsets that were painted on the sky each night as the sun sunk out of sight. We feasted on all the fruits of the sea, lobsters, clams and freshly caught bluefish. We gathered home grown vegetables that were put out at the edge of people's lawns to sell and had a wonderful time. We hunted for and collected beach plums and choke cherries to turn into juice and freeze to take home to make luscious jelly for the winter. On rainy days there were jigsaw puzzles, Scrabble, drawing and painting and favorite books to read. We stopped the world and got off for two glorious weeks – no TV, no newspapers, mail, telephone or any modern appliances – life became very simple. The sea breeze was our dryer and the laundry was hung on the line and billowed in the wind.

The years went by, the boys grew up, went off to College and left home. Whenever they could they joined us at the Cape. One year, our son Ian, who was living in Boston, told us he had bought his own little cottage so that a part of the Cape could be his own. We were all very excited and when we saw this diminutive little two bedroom dollhouse, bordered by a split rail fence and set in a little pine grove, we knew there was work to do. We painted, plastered, insulated, made curtains and pillows and soon it was a charmer. One year Ian invited us all to spend Thanksgiving at the Cape. We cooked most of the dinner at home and froze it for its journey to the Cape. How we ever fitted four grown men, their parents, a cat and a dog that did not get on, into that little dollhouse I will never know – but we did. All too soon our holiday came to an end and with great reluctance we packed up the car to return to New York. As we neared home the air became thick and heavy, the sky cloudy and dull and the noise and houses seem to crowd in on us. The spell was broken.

Ian now has three houses at the Cape, each one larger and more luxurious than the last, but none fill us with the joy the first little cottage did. We still try to visit the Cape each year before the summer visitors arrive or after they leave. It never changes and each year we recharge the internal batteries that lift our spirits with memories for the coming year.

One loves one's children unconditionally but as well as a lot of pride and joy one of them can bring pain and unhappiness into your life. Although we love them we do not always agree or like what they do. It hurts to see them in bad situations and one feels so helpless to have to stand by and watch them struggle with their problems and have your help rejected. With a united front the pain and worry is eased.

The Treasure Box

Time marches on and adds the years relentlessly no matter what else is happening. The ravages of old age sometimes rob the memory, dim the eyesight and dull the hearing and much patience is required. Sometimes more patience than one can muster …which give cause for tensions in a marriage to mount. I really don't feel any different to what I did 25 years ago. Maybe I have gained a little more wisdom and have a lot more aches and pains. I have lived through many wars, seen many births and deaths, many marriages and divorces, many changes in the world and much happiness and sadness.

Marriage is like a patchwork quilt made up of many squares coming from all directions – some bright and happy, some drab and sad but the kaleidoscope when all are joined together makes a unique life made up of many memories. Thankfully it is the drab squares that are not always added to the quilt and forgotten and only the brilliant shiny ones that are added to enjoy. It takes time and patience to create a masterpiece. Some of the patches have ragged edges and need more work. Piecing it all together is a laborious chore but finally there is a beautiful piece of work that will surround you with comfort, warmth and the knowledge that you are protected from the cold. The same rules apply to marriage. When patches get worn and thin it is time to get out the needle and repair them even though sometimes it is an unwelcome chore. When the edges are not perfect more care and patience is needed.

This Christmas I had an interesting gift from a dear friend in England. It was beautifully gift wrapped and as I tore open the wrapping I wondered what was inside. I found an exquisite box that had originated in Paris – it looked as though it should be adorning a Victorian ladies boudoir. Covered in the palest pastel shell pink silk, it was embellished with lace, gold thread and silk ribbon roses. It was truly a work of art. I carefully removed the lid to see what was inside. I looked into a box that was lined in pale pink padded satin and was empty.

When I thanked my friend she told me it was a box to hold my precious treasures. I was rather taken aback as I have no material treasures, I do not want any material treasures and I do not need any material treasures. For my treasures would never fit into that beautiful box and could not be seen if they were there. My precious treasures are the valuable friendships of family and friends and the love that has endured for over half a century and is as bright as ever. It is the treasure of knowing that I can paint and have been able to show other people how to put their feelings on paper and value the beauty of nature, see the Technicolor sunsets, experience the serenity of a peaceful summer beach and the wonder of silence in a snowy winter scene. It is a treasure to remember my children's early days and the pleasure they brought us and the fact that we have lived in the same house for 55 years. All of these treasures could never fit into that beautiful box. So if you look into my box and see it empty you will be seeing a different box to what I will see, a box spilling over with memories and treasures of a lifetime.

We are tested many times over the years and have many heart aches to endure. On our Golden wedding we decided to go on a Caribbean cruise. We had never been on a cruise before and the planning was exciting. A few days before we were to leave we had a call from Boston to say that our dearest son Chris was to undergo serious emergency cancer surgery that night. We cancelled our cruise and spent our Golden Wedding day in the ICU with Chris. We never thought he would survive the surgery and it was one of the best gifts we could have been given to be able to spend the day with him. We never did go on that cruise. Two years later Black Tuesday came.

That morning in August was filled with brilliant sunshine and foreboded another scorching hot day. We were wakened by the ringing of the telephone. A voice from the hospital was telling us that our beautiful Christopher had died. A dense, deep black shroud descended and wrapped itself around us closing out the sun, the warmth, the sounds and even the air was stifling. We were cut off from the whole world. Black Tuesday - the day that changed our lives forever… A piece of each of us died that day but we still had each other.

As age slows us down our thoughts travel back through the paths of time and we recall all the happiness throughout the last 60 years. We enjoyed some of the same things yet we had our own special hobbies. Morton's first love was sailing and he was never happier than sailing around Long Island Sound. I don't like sailing at all so was quite content to go with a friend and spend the time with my watercolors. We both enjoyed volunteering so together we became docents at a large historic estate on Long Island's North Shore. We have volunteered at the local hospital for the last twenty years – both in different departments and find it most rewarding.

Sadly, this last Thanksgiving week my best friend and better half departed from this earthly world. I have shared more than sixty years with Morton, a gentle, compassionate and loving man who gave me security, peace and happiness for so many years. My life became aimless, bleak and lonely but I feel blessed to have been part of Morton's life for so long.

With openness, trust, truthfulness and love it is possible to enjoy life to the fullest with the one that stepped off a bus into your life on a foggy day in London town so many years ago.

THE SECRET TO GLADYS AND MORTON'S MARRIAGE?

THE POWER OF FOOD

Of course, in that foggy afternoon in the London of 1939, it had to start around a cup of tea, but, alas, no finger sandwiches to accompany the ritual… Poor Gladys, a young woman who had just graduated from the prestigious London School of Home Economics, was not quite sure how this dashing American officer would deal with the lack of proper British decorum: "As I look back, I do not know how anybody managed to survive on the meager amount of food we were allowed".

Obviously, it did not deter young Morton who finally persuaded his British girl-friend to jump over the "puddle "and join him in matrimony in the daunting New World. They were married in Chicago in a frigid snowstorm in the beginning of January 1950. Gladys describes the ceremony as "a somber affair with a few family members dressed in black". She overheard Morton's father saying" it would never last". Gladys found herself isolated, without friends and without any members of her beloved English family. Morton quickly found a job at CBS in the Special Effects Department, a great opportunity, exciting and unpredictable. "The long and irregular hours of Morton's schedule were very hard on the rest of the family. With four small boys and a house to look after and no help, support group or family, I often wonder how I survived."

Gladys knew she had to survive, she had to be there for her husband and for her children. So she built her life back, utilizing those skills she had learned in happier days in England. "I worked as a food stylist, a food editor and later created some cookbooks for a hospital and church as a volunteer contribution. I loved my work and still try out and create new recipes each week for my family."

Gladys knew that food could be the magic element that would keep her family together. Food, like music and sex, releases in our blood a powerful brain neurotransmitter called dopamine. Sharing this physiological dopamine release response with your family and friends during a meal creates a pleasurable feeling. Julia Child, the famous chef, observed:" Dining with one's friends and beloved family is certainly one of life's primal and most innocent delights, one that is both soul-satisfying and eternal." Oprah Winfrey described the joy of eating with friends somewhat differently: "My idea of heaven is a great big baked potato and someone to share it with! ".

Regardless of one's own cultural, religious and ethnic background, we all remember family gatherings around the dining room table to celebrate holidays and events. In her excellent book, The Surprising Power of Family Meals: How Eating Together Makes Us Smarter, Stronger, Healthier and Happier (2005), Miriam Weinstein explains the function of the family meal : "Supper is only the occasion, the excuse. The subject is actually family — establishing, enjoying, and maintaining ties. The goal is creating and reinforcing a secure place for your loved ones in a society that can seem awfully uninterested in human needs."

Food became the focus and the bond for Gladys and Morton's family. Nowhere did they feel happier and more fulfilled as a couple than when the whole family drove to Cape Cod to vacation together. No more tensions, no more long hours waiting alone in the kitchen for the husband to return... As she tells the story of her life with Morton, with all the joyful memories as well as with the tragedies they both shared, nowhere does she express herself with more happiness than when she writes about Cape Cod. Love bloomed in their little cottage by the sea. There, she could truly indulge in her passion and express her love for her family using food as a vector:" We feasted on all the fruits of the sea, lobsters, clams and freshly caught bluefish. We gathered home grown vegetables that were put out at the edge of people's lawns to sell and had a wonderful time. We hunted for and collected beach plums and choke cherries to turn into juice and freeze to take home to make luscious jelly for the winter."

As the years passed, one of their sons, Ian, built a second summer cottage on Cape Cod. To celebrate, he invited his parents to spend Thanksgiving at the Cape. Gladys knew exactly what she wanted to do for her family on that special occasion: "We cooked most of the dinner at home and froze it for its journey to the Cape."

Oh yes... Gladys and Morton shared many wonderful meals together for over sixty years until the one very last family reunion. And it was written that their last meal should be a Thanksgiving dinner, where they could one last time express together their gratitude for all the foods they had shared as a couple and as a family: "Sadly, this last Thanksgiving week my best friend and better half departed from this earthly world. I have shared more than sixty years with Morton, a gentle, compassionate and loving man who gave me security, peace and happiness for so many years."

Nowadays, Gladys bakes wonderful chocolate and vanilla meringues for her friends, but she no longer cooks family meals...

CHAPTER IV

Marvin and Elise (60 years)

"Forever and a Day..."

It doesn't seem possible that on June 15th Marvin and I will be celebrating our 60th Wedding Anniversary. The years just flew by and the "young marrieds" in 1954 are now the older generation.

I look at our three children, who are all married and our nine grand-children and I think "Wait a minute! We are just beginning!..." We have so much yet to do and there aren't enough hours in the day to get it all done...

Therefore, Marvin and I have adopted the "Carpe Diem" philosophy: Seize the day and make the moments count, every day lived more abundantly than the day before.

Marvin and I have grown together at each stage of our lives. We know each other since we were children, living around the corner from one another. We went to the same public school in the Bronx, in an area called Highbridge, located six blocks from Yankee Stadium.

Marvin is the eldest of three brothers. I was the class monitor for the second grade and guided the students, including his younger brothers, each day from schoolyard to classroom. We had the best of all worlds. We shared common interests, friends, teachers, respect for one another and respect for our parents.

In our neighborhood, there were a few hangouts where we would all gather after school or after dinner. One was situated right in front of the apartment houses. Our favorite was at the "top of the hill"...and there were many, many hills! The area had two separate flights of twelve stairs to get from our block to the playground below. That playground is now the new Yankee Stadium. Years later, whenever we would go on trips and people would complain about climbing up a hill, we would answer: "You want to see hills? Come to Highbridge in the Bronx!"

Another popular gathering place was the candy store, the only place you could buy bubble gum during World War II. The owner of the store had two boys who belonged to our group. So, even though we always blocked the entrance of the store, we were usually allowed to gather there, at least most of the time. We are talking about twenty noisy teenagers lolling around!...

Marvin and I were platonic friends until I was 17 and a half. Our first date as a couple took place at the arcade in City Island, on July 11, 1951. Our second date was even more special. Marvin invited me to the Aquacade in Flushing Meadow, the site of the 1939 World's Fair. I wore a hand-me-down black and white silk polka dot dress, lent by my cousin, and very uncomfortable narrow shoes given to me by my aunt. Marvin wore a hand-me-down green and orange glen-plaid suit from his uncle. We were quite the stylish couple!

One day, we decided to open a bank account to save our pennies. We literally "saved" pennies, placed them in a green pencil case and marched off to the bank. At the desk, I unlocked the case to count them. Yes, you guessed it, all the pennies spilled all over the floor of the bank in every direction. Slightly embarrassed… We were told that the pennies had to be rolled. Never forgot it.

I was an only child. My Mom was the youngest of ten children and my Dad was the eldest of ten children. Many cousins, aunts and uncles… Always surrounded by family, even though the relatives lived in Brooklyn and Long Island…

My Mom came from an Orthodox Russian Jewish family and my Dad, a mould maker and sculptor, was from an Italian Roman Catholic family. I was raised Jewish and my Dad converted to Judaism. My Mother's family sat "shiva" for her when she married my Dad. It wasn't until three years later that the family relented. My grandmother finally acknowledged that Paul, my Dad, was the best son-in-law she could have ever dreamt of.

Holidays were interesting. We celebrated all of them. At the time, I did not realize that this was a life experience in the making. I got to understand first-hand the differences and similarities of Judaism and Catholicism. For many years, I was ashamed of my maiden name. I eventually became very proud of my heritage as I matured.

My parents adored Marvin. They thought he was so special -brilliant, compassionate and loving. They said he must be from "Mars". I was equally fond of my in-laws and I always felt that I have two mothers. Both my mother-in-law and my father-in -law were attorneys, a rare and remarkable achievement in those days. There were three women in her class. She would walk to class on Saturdays and request that another student take notes since she observed the Sabbath. When Marvin and I were about to be married, his Mom consulted with his grandmother to explore potential objections to our union, since I came from a mixed marriage. After checking with a Rabbi, Grandma Rose replied that I was like a daughter to her. She would be very happy to see us married.

Marvin completed his college at New York University undergraduate. He later attended New York University Law School, as had his parents before him and one of our daughters later on. In college, he had enrolled in ROTC. Upon graduation, he wanted to serve his army obligation before embarking in his Law studies.

It was the end of the Korean War. He traveled to The Pentagon to request a European assignment. When he received his marching orders to go to Germany, he asked me to join him. We had just become engaged. Three weeks after our big engagement party in my parent's apartment, where we had removed all the furniture to another room in order to accommodate our guests, we were married on a Tuesday night in June. It was the only night available for the gathering and tradition says that Tuesdays weddings bring luck. It was a relatively small wedding of eighty people. Off to Europe we went! I would finish Hunter College upon my return and Marvin would eventually get to Law School, where he was the valedictorian of his class.

Marvin was 22 and I was 20. We grew up in the Depression Years. Employment for my Dad included the Work Projects Administration (WPA), the largest New Deal agency, established in 1935. Marvin's parents had a very modest law practice and were always trying to drum up business. They shared a suite of offices in New York City. Clients were hard to find. One of the lawyers in the suite represented the Lutheran churches. My mother-in-law served as an official witness when the Lutheran churches' clients drew their wills. She had such an engaging personality! When the lawyer responsible for the Lutheran churches died, all his clients came to her for professional advice. In fact, many of them spoke along with our Rabbi, at her funeral.

Europe was an eye opener for us. Army life introduced us to another segment of the real world. People from every state in the union…Different ethics, different ideas about politics and religion.

Marvin, without a law degree to his name for the moment, was the legal officer for the regiment. He was the liaison officer between the post and the town. For my part, I was assigned a Kindergarten class for the Army children, since I was studying Early Childhood Education. One night a week, I would teach the GI's how to read and write. Literacy was a requirement for those soldiers who wanted to make the Army their career. I also had a Girl Scout troop. Once, I wrote a Holiday Play for the Army Post and invited the local German citizens and the Mayor of the town.

Friday nights, Marvin would conduct services for the Jewish soldiers in the vestry room of the church since there was no Chaplain and I would make the Oneg Shabbat.

Living away from well- meaning relatives during the first fourteen months of our married life allowed us to mature and adjust to our new situation as a couple... After our return from Europe, having experienced the luxurious freedom and the ability to travel every weekend, holiday and leave time, we faced a new unexpected challenge: keeping both sides of the family happy! What to do about Thanksgiving? Whose house will it be for Pesach?

Solved it! All family gatherings would always take place in our home- whether it was a tiny apartment in Washington Heights with a kitchen built into a small wall of the living room or any other home we would subsequently live in. Twenty to thirty guests would be the norm.

Another challenge was succeeding in stretching my meager teacher's salary without putting a burden on our parents whose means were quite limited. I finished Hunter College and got a teaching position in Yonkers. Had to split my time… Morning in one school, afternoon in another… There were many times that the two miles walk from one school to the other was necessary since pennies were saved for exceptional carfare in trains or buses.

Needless to say, we did not own a car. Besides, I did not learn to drive until our son was two and a half, five years after we were married. One time, when our daughter, born in 1957, was ill, we could not even afford the $20.00 needed to pay for a doctor's visit.

Life is a test. We are meant to be challenged. Healthy discussions and bringing a problem to the surface is really the path to walk. Anger, hate, hostility and jealousy are a waste of time. Ralph Waldo Emerson said: "For every minute of anger, you lose sixty seconds of happiness". I have framed his statement in our kitchen as an everyday reminder of the secret of happiness.

Marvin and I have always understood each other, using eye contact, facial expression or other body language. This new language, this communication process requires time, patience, smiles and compromise. The magic recipe varies, sometimes 50/50, other times 60/40 or even 90/10!

What is the toughest moment in a relationship? For some, it's the seven year itch. For some it's midlife: Who am I? Where am I going? For us, it was none of the above. Our lives were so involved with caring for parents, raising children to be independent, providing secular and religious education and community responsibility not to mention making a living and improving the quality of our lives. Foundations had to be established for our family. What the children chose to do once they reached adulthood was to be their choice, as long as it was an honest living.

The toughest moment occurred in 1984. After thirty years of blessed marital life, Marvin was diagnosed with Chronic Lymphatic Leukemia. He did his research. He chose a physician at MD Anderson Cancer Center in Houston, Texas. This doctor used biological alternatives rather than chemotherapy as treatment approach. Our feeling was that one could always start with biological therapies and add chemotherapy later if needed.

At the time, the prognosis was a two to three life expectancy. Fortunately, twenty-eight years have passed… Marvin is feeling better than ever.

This was a difficult time. We had to travel to Houston every three to six months, getting a treatment, and dealing with stress and anxiety filled years. Of course, a positive attitude is more than half of the healing process. Through the ordeal, Marvin has learned counseling techniques to guide many people along the way. He helps them realize that, in the storms of life, a positive attitude with smiles and laughter can get you through the tears.

Marvin also believes that you should do your homework. You should learn everything you can about the illness and be prepared to ask questions. An informed patient is at an advantage. It was then, back in 1984, that we realized the wisdom of Dr. Wayne Dyer: "If you change the way you look at things, the things you look at change".

The Secret: Think positive thoughts! Negative thoughts use too much valuable energy and waste valuable time. We were able to cope early in our lives. We matured and learned each day from one another and from everyone we meet, from the storekeeper to the captains of industry. A doorman once recently told us: "Inch by Inch is a cinch; Yard by Yard is hard".

One of the positive things in this stage of our development is spending quality time separately with each of the grandchildren. Some of the grandchildren are adults already, (funny how that works that we stay the same) and keeping up with their 21st century ideas is not only stimulating but very enjoyable. We love to seek their advice on computer glitches or is it our own glitch trying to make head or tail of why the machine responds or doesn't respond.

Would we do it again? ABSOLUTELY!

- Advice-
- Extreme patience
- Compassion
- Role reversal - What is it like for your partner in a situation
- Don't expect 50-50 - The equation changes with each situation
- Respect one another
- Don't interrupt
- Not necessary to get in the last word unless it is I Love You
- Never go to sleep angry
- It is okay to be silly now and then

THE SECRET TO MARVIN AND ELISE'S MARRIAGE?

THE POWER OF SPIRITUALITY

Elise and Marvin grew up together, living around the corner from one another an attending the same public school in the Bronx, six blocks from Yankee Stadium. Yet their backgrounds were quite different: Elise was an only child. Her mother came from an Orthodox Russian Jewish family and her father, a mould maker and sculptor, was from an Italian Roman Catholic family... A real tragedy for her maternal grandparents, who literally sat "shiva" when their daughter insisted on marrying out of the faith! Her father had to convert to Judaism and Elise's parents agreed to raise their daughter in the Jewish faith.

This religious upbringing left its marks on Elise: "Holidays were interesting. We celebrated all of them. At the time, I did not realize that this was a life experience in the making. I got to understand first- hand the differences and similarities of Judaism and Catholicism. For many years, I was ashamed of my maiden name. I eventually became very proud of my heritage as I matured. "

For his part, Marvin was raised by parents who were both attorneys, "a rare and remarkable achievement in those days... They shared a suite of offices in New York City... One of the lawyers in the suite represented the Lutheran churches. Marvin's mother served as an official witness when the Lutheran s clients drew their wills...When the lawyer responsible for the Lutheran churches died, all his clients came to her for professional advice."

When Marvin informed his parents that he wanted to marry Elise, Marvin's mother asked her own mother for advice "to explore potential objections to our union, since Elise came from a mixed marriage. After checking with a Rabbi, Grandma Rose replied that Elise was like a daughter to her. She would be very happy to see us married."

So, with the blessing of all four parents, Elise and Marvin did get married, shortly after Marvin had received his marching orders to go to Germany, to serve his army obligation as a ROTC undergraduate student at New York University, before embarking in his Law studies. Spirituality continue to sustain the newlyweds in Europe: "Friday nights, Marvin would conduct services for the Jewish soldiers in the vestry room of the church since there was no Chaplain and I would make the Oneg Shabbat. Elise, for her part, would teach a Kindergarten class for the Army children, and a literacy class for soldiers, since she was studying Early Childhood Education. She wrote a Holiday Play for the Army Post and invited the local German citizens and the Mayor of the town. "Europe was an eye opener for us. Army life introduced us to another segment of the real world. People from every state in the union... Different ethics, different ideas about politics and religion."

The real, unexpected, challenge awaited the young couple upon their return to the US:" Keeping both sides of the family happy! What to do about Thanksgiving? Whose house will it be for Pesach?"

Marvin and Elise were born problem-solvers! "All family gatherings would always take place in our home-whether it was a tiny apartment in Washington Heights with a kitchen built into a small wall of the living room or any other home we would subsequently live in. Twenty to thirty guests would be the norm".

In a 2003 NIH report, Linda J. Waite and Evelyn L. Lehrer analyze and compare the Benefits from Marriage and Religion in the United States (Popul Dev Rev. 2003 June; 29(2): 255–276). They state:" America is a religious nation. The vast majority of Americans, when asked, profess a belief in God and affirm that religion is at least "fairly important" in their lives; about 60 percent of the population report membership in a religious organization and 45 percent state that they attend religious services at least monthly. Most American adults are currently married and almost all will marry at some time in their lives... We compare religion and marriage as social institutions, both clearly on everyone's short list of "most important institutions." Marital unions differ in a multitude of ways, including the characteristics, such as education, earnings, religion, and cultural background, of each of the partners, and the homogamy of their match on these characteristics. Similarly, religion has multiple aspects. Both marriage and religiosity generally have far-reaching, positive effects; that they influence similar domains of life; and that there are important parallels in the pathways through which each achieves these outcomes."

They conclude: "Marriage and religion influence various dimensions of life, including physical health and longevity, mental health and happiness, economic well-being, and the raising of children."

Elise and Marvin would surely agree with these researchers. Rather than allow religion and spirituality to draw them apart, the two of them openly embraced the richness of the cultural heritages and grew strength together as a couple, respecting their own spiritual lives and welcoming with open arms new ideas and unfamiliar traditions." We matured and learned each day from one another and from everyone we meet, from the storekeeper to the captains of industry"

Elise and Marvin are still enjoying each other's companies, travelling, writing and celebrating family traditions with their children and grandchildren and friends, their doorman and their business partners.

CHAPTER V

Rhona and Desmond (59 years)

"From Guyana to Tennessee"
By Rhona Carrington

My life began in a little village, Agricola, in Guyana, known then as British Guiana, a small colony in South America. As an only child, I always enjoyed my Anglican school, and welcomed the socialization offered in its nurturing setting.

When I was sixteen, I started teaching at the Village Public School. However, as I approached the mature age of eighteen, it dawned on me that none of my colleague female teachers were married! I did want to get married and have children of my own! To my Mother's great concern, after two years, I pursued employment with the Civil Service and was assigned to the Registry of Courts, in the capital city of Georgetown, two and a half miles away from my village. In those days, the most popular and the most convenient mode of transportation was either the bus or your own bicycle. In fact, you would have been very proud to own one of those bicycles!

One day, after work, I went on my bicycle to visit a friend. There, I saw for the very first time my future husband! He seemed unusually shy, handsome, but much too quiet and reserved for my taste...All we said to each other was "Hello" and then "Good-bye".

About eight months later, I was invited to a birthday party at my friend's house. Here he was again, standing outside, by the entrance. I ventured to invite him inside: "Aren't you coming in?" His response was awkward: "Does it matter?"... I thought him particularly rude and snapped back at him: "Not particularly!" I decided to forget about him and enjoy my evening! As the night progressed, I was happily dancing with a delightful young man. However, my dance partner proceeded gently to hand me over, on the dance floor, to the discourteous individual who had offended me earlier. Well, I decided to give him an opportunity to apologize for his peculiar remark...As we danced on, the music suddenly stopped. It was midnight. A whistle blew from outdoors, the signal that my girlfriend's brother had arrived to escort us safely home, back to our little village. Desmond was still holding my hands and didn't let go when I explained that my escort had arrived and I needed to leave at once! He did the unthinkable! He firmly planted a kiss on my lips in front of everyone! I was so embarrassed that I literally pulled myself away and ran down the stairs, never to return to this awful house!

All week-end, I thought of the dreadful adventure: I wouldn't say a word to anyone in my village, because this behavior was considered a violation of a young lady's rights and privacy. However, by Monday, after work, I felt I should return to the house and discuss with my friend the events which had occurred last Saturday evening. To my amazement, she erupted in laughter and called in her mother. Her comment was "Do you mean *our* Desmond, next door?" I just realized he was their neighbor. I was trapped!

Now I couldn't possibly leave their house until darkness! I also knew that I should avoid visiting this house in the future at all costs.

Alas…He did catch up with me on his bicycle, a few weeks later, as I was riding back from work. He invited me to see a movie with him the following Thursday. Something about him was intriguing, even though I had plenty of friends around me. I decided to give him yet another chance. After all, I enjoyed movies as well and so no major reason to miss an opportunity!

As I was preparing myself for the evening, I found out through a friend that he had recently taken a relative of mine, a girl from my village, to a show in town over the week-end. Frankly, this guy was too much trouble for me! I decided to stand him up and to stay comfortably at home in my pajamas rather than make a fool of myself at the movies in his company! I settled in, listening to the news on the radio (we had no television back then), when I heard a knock at the door. It was Desmond.

His first reaction, seeing me in my pajamas, was of one of fright. Was I ill? I explained that I had become aware of his outing with a relative of mine and had no interest in pursuing a relationship in those circumstances. He quickly and convincingly cleared the misunderstanding. She was a mutual friend, not a date. He also knew that I could not have reached him to cancel our movie date. In 1949, very few homes had a telephone!

As time went on, Desmond discovered that I love having friends around. Nothing makes me happier than social gatherings! He, on the other hand, is very reserved, preferring intimate settings. This difference created quite a bit of friction between us…One day he invited me to a picnic. I was delighted with the idea, which would finally give me the opportunity to meet some of his own friends. When we reached the picnic spot, I discovered to my horror that there was nobody there! He admitted that he had organized a picnic…for two! I was fit to be tied, but survived the day.

Desmond's determination and devotion finally won me over. During his time in college, in Guiana, he learned gardening. To the delight of my mother, he brought me a beautiful rose plant. My mother's hobby was to raise rabbits. Desmond and my mother became great pals, discussing rabbits and gardening under the hot sun of Guiana.

The months of friendships became years. One day, Desmond, who had been working as a laboratory technician at school, told me of his plans to go abroad and study Medicine. His mother was a midwife in our country. She had a dream for her son…She wanted him to become a doctor. I loved his plans and welcomed her support: Going "abroad" meant, of course, leaving Guiana and going to England or perhaps to Ireland, to attend University, as others of our friends had done. I also had my own dream: I wanted to join the World Health Organization in England. Once on board, I would get to travel to different international assignments. What a perfect life it would be for each of us!

Unbeknownst to us, his godfather decided to sponsor him to attend medical school in the United States of America…A most generous offer, but not quite what either of us had in mind…I didn't know what to think. In September of 1952, Desmond left Guiana …I was alone.

Shortly after Desmond left, I attended a friend's party and met a very nice young man who promptly asked me out on a date. Before I even realized what I was saying, I declined and told him that I was actually engaged to someone who had left for the USA. This young man was charming. He liked dancing, and singing. He particularly enjoyed the Nat King Cole's records which I so loved. Before long, he suggested that I write Desmond a "Dear John" letter. Deep down, I realized I would never be able to write that letter. On the contrary, I resolved to travel to the USA at my first opportunity, which was my upcoming annual vacation. I arrived in New York in December 1953. Two weeks later, we were married in Brooklyn. None of my family members were in attendance, I was alone, resolute, though scared. It was a small and beautiful wedding. To this day, I cherish the memory of that day and bless all those who made it possible. I returned back to Guiana, a married woman.

After one year, I finally resigned from my job as a county clerk in Georgetown and returned to New York to seek permanent residency. Our life had a simple, humble beginning, in a small studio room where we lived happily for four years. During those four years, my father died in Guiana and I brought my widowed mother to live with us, since I had no siblings to care after her. I had given birth to our daughter and soon afterward was expecting a second child (our son), when we received the news that my husband had been accepted in medical school in Nashville Tennessee. This news meant that he would be spending the next five years in the South, away from his wife and his young children. I now had to shoulder the full responsibility to care for myself, my mother and our two children. My mother was a strong asset to me. She encouraged me with words of wisdom which still resonate with me to this day.

The years that followed were challenging to say the least! After my husband finished his internship and his residency, he found a position at Kings County Hospital Center in Brooklyn. He remained there for the next 24 years, becoming the Director of the Home Care Division, while operating his private office in our house in Brooklyn. I join him to assist in the daily operation of the practice. Our children were now teenagers and doing very well at school. My daughter eventually attended Amherst College and my son, Brooklyn College. Desmond and I are very proud of them…Our only difficult times were the ones generated by my in-laws. Of course, they were rightly proud of their son's achievement and professional success. Somehow, they forgot, or chose not to recognize, the sacrifices that others made to pave his road to success…My mother-in-law once told me:" Rhona, you are young and you can wait to get his full attention. We need him now!" Our two young children did not get to spend much time with their father, working six days a week and then rushing to his own parents on Sundays. I resented my in-laws' pressure on Desmond and their unrealistic expectations. Eventually, I insisted on getting more time for me and for the children, which created unnecessary tensions.

Strange that I should be so content with the simple life that filled all my dreams…My only painful and difficult years were the ones I spent alone with my two small children and my widowed mother. She was, like myself, a stranger to the values and routine of the American way of life. Everything here was so fast paced, not allowing anyone any spare time to establish lasting friendships and relationships. For my part, I clung to a small group of folks from my country and neighboring West Indian Islanders. Together, we would reminisce and relive our years in our beloved old world. I found that our values were quite different: we needed money, yes, to survive, but friendships and devotion to a cause were always more important.

Along with this adjustment challenge, I also had to figure out how to best deal with my in-laws. Neither of them ever offered, or assisted, or even encouraged me, in the raising of the young ones. When Desmond received his doctor's degree, they expected me to step aside and make room for his new patients. Whenever a conflict would arise, they suspected my negative influence. Naturally, their attitude created a permanent degree of tension in our home. My husband felt a constant need to protect me from his own parents. In reality, he worked five days at the hospital and all day Saturday in his private office. Our only day together, with our children, was Sunday. However, on Sundays, he was clearly expected to visit his mother in her home, even though she could easily have come to spend that day with us. She was so very proud of her son who had achieved the dream she had hoped for all her life… Off he went, every week-end, rain or shine, with the two children in tow. Little by little, the children became very reluctant to travel to their grandmother every week. They resented being stuck in front of a television while their father – whom they hadn't seen all week - was having private discussions with their selfish grandmother. I managed somehow to keep my resentment to myself for all these years and am grateful that I didn't say anything that I would have regretted later on.

My own mother, on the other hand, was a simple Chinese woman who had enjoyed raising her grandchildren, the pride and joy of her life, until the ripe old age of 94! Her philosophy was very plain:"Love and help those less fortunate than you are". Her only flaw in my eyes was her need to refer to my treasured collection of crystals, chinas and antiques as "a pack of junk". Today, I have finally come to see her point of view because I no longer have the patience or energy to dust and wash my "pack of junk"! So if you are interested in acquiring an eclectic collection of "junk", do come by my house and stand on line, in case neither my daughter nor her children want to inherit this collection!

After all is said and done, I wouldn't trade my life for anything! We are now both 82 years old. As Desmond ages, I have become his caregiver and I am grateful to God and to our many friends for their support. My former boss, twenty years after my retirement as a secretary from his leather-good company, still keeps in touch at holidays…

Marriage is a deep, life-long commitment. Marriage should be entered only if there is true love. Since no one is perfect, we should all learn to forgive and forget.

THE SECRET TO DESMOND AND RHONA'S MARRIAGE?

THE POWER OF EDUCATION

Back then, in British Guyana, in a little village called Agricola, a very young Rhona was enjoying her Anglican school, and looking forward to teaching at the Village Public School. Little did she know that not too far away, lived a young laboratory technician by the name of Desmond who was nurturing two dreams: he wanted to go abroad and study Medicine and ...he wanted to marry her!

Once Desmond mastered the courage to approach her, Rhona became actually enthralled with the whole idea: "Going "abroad" meant, of course, leaving Guyana and going to England or perhaps to Ireland, to attend University, as others of our friends had done. I also had my own dream: I wanted to join the World Health Organization in England. Once on board, I would get to travel to different international assignments. What a perfect life it would be for each of us!"

Rhona and Desmond were determined to receive a high level education. They could not have realized, as they embarked on their life as a young couple, the sacrifices they would have to make together to succeed:" Unbeknownst to us, his godfather decided to sponsor him to attend medical school in the United States of America...A most generous offer, but not quite what either of us had in mind...I didn't know what to think. In September of 1952, Desmond left Guiana ...I was alone...The years that followed were challenging to say the least! After my husband finished his internship and his residency, he found a position at Kings County Hospital Center in Brooklyn. ⁰

Education is a powerful tool. Desmond had succeeded! He was now recognized by his colleagues and his peers as an exceptional physician and was given a full-time position at Kings County Hospital. For the next 24 years, he would serve as the Director of the Home Care Division, while operating a private practice office in their Brooklyn home. Meanwhile, Rhona would use her skills and her training to assist him and to raise the children who were becoming scholars of their own.

Successful marriages, as Rhona and Desmond's union, have been shown to be linked to greater professional achievement as well as happiness, better health, longevity, and better incomes. The National Marriage Project recently reported on the benefits of higher education not only on career success and financial benefits, but perhaps, more importantly, on marital bliss! Based on current national data, Americans who have completed a college education have a higher marriage success rate than those who have only received a high school diploma.

Elaine Rose, at the University of Washington, coined the expression «the success gap» referring to the negative correlation between women educa-tion and likelihood to get married. New data from the 1990 and 2000 U.S. census data indicate that the success gap is actually shrinking:" In 1980, a woman with three years of graduate school was 13 percent less likely to be married than a woman with only a high-school diploma. By 2000, that gap shrank to less than 5 percent» said Rose. Furthermore, divorce rates among college graduates have been decreasing. Finally, 54% of American with high school education have had a child out-of-wedlock, compared with only 6 percent of college graduates. A study from the University of Pennsylvania's Wharton School, analyzing marriage data from the Census and the 2008 American Community Survey, found that college educated women are the least likely to divorce, while women who drop out of high school are the least likely to marry. Educated women are also more likely to report being happy in their marriages than less educated women, the report concluded.

Desmond is no longer a physician. He has become a patient. Despite all the sacrifices that so many years of education required for both of them and for their children, Rhona is still very happy in her marriage:" After all is said and done, I wouldn't trade my life for anything! We are now both 82 years old. As Desmond ages, I have become his caregiver and I am grateful to

God and to our many friends for their support". She continues to care for him as she has done for the past 59 years, attentive to his every need and grateful for the privilege of spending yet one more day with the man she loves and admires so much.

CHAPTER VI

Sallie and Sherwood (56 years)

"It Was a Hot Saturday Night in July..."
By Sallie Newman

It was a hot Saturday night in July, the kind where whatever you put on sticks to you, because your body is covered with a sheen of perspiration that just won't disappear. Reluctantly, I was getting ready for yet another blind date. They all seem to be so boring, or worse, obnoxious.

Cousin Davey thought the guy who lived on the first floor of his apartment building would be a likely candidate to meet me...On the other hand, his wife didn't think I would be interested...What was she thinking?

Sherwood showed up on time, looked okay, except for those brown wing-tipped shoes!

We had a pleasant time, but no bells and whistles. At the end of the evening, he asked if we could see each other the following weekend and I told him I might go to visit my brother in Connecticut. It was a shameful lie, but you must realize that those were the days when you played games with prospective dates. You played hard to get. You were not supposed to be readily available.

I had no such plans, and Sherwood was ever focused on what he wanted. He said he would call during the week to see if we could get together. When I got home that evening, my Mom asked how the evening went and I replied, "Mom, he wore brown shoes!"

I still don't know what I had against his shoes. After all, I have a few pair of brown shoes myself. I guess it was my way of expressing a lack of chemistry.

We did see each other the next weekend, and the next, and I soon found out what a wonderful guy he was. I discovered that he was sweet, generous and respectful. Whenever I met a friend or acquaintance of his, they always remarked that he was this great guy who would bend over backwards to help anyone, whether they needed help or not. He proved himself to be a wonderful suitor. Once I stopped playing the game, I started to hear the bells and whistles, and before long we knew that we were meant to be!

We discussed getting married and said we wanted a small intimate wedding…no conspicuous consumption.

Our parents thought differently, they wanted to share their happiness with friends and family. They relished the thought of basking in the loving glow that we felt for each other. So a wedding was planned and indeed we all enjoyed the simcha!

At our wedding reception, we received a precious bit of advice from a dear friend. "Most people think marriage is a "50 – 50" deal, but it's really "100 – 100", each of you giving all to the other. The magic formula worked.

"100 – 100" has been our motto throughout our married life, and to this day we still give completely to each other.

I was teaching school, and Sherwood was getting a lot of overtime at his job as an electrician, so Sherwood suggested we buy a house. We had saved some money and could afford a small house. It would be a good beginning for our life together.

We both lived with our parents until we were married, and neither lived in a house. Apartment living is all we ever knew, but we went about looking for our home. The first house had a dishwasher, and I was ready to buy it…I never had a dishwasher. It was a bad layout and a terrible home, but Sherwood said whatever home we bought, we could have a dishwasher…The second home we saw was smelly and moldy, and I asked the realtor who would ever live in a home like that. She replied that if you bought that home, you would naturally tear it down and build new. The third house we saw was our little dream house. Just right for a newly married couple with a child on the way…

Carrie was born nine months after our wedding and we were off on the adventure that was parenthood. She was sweet, ate well, slept well and she filled our days with awe.

Two years later, Andrea was born and she too filled our need to love and nurture.

I resigned from teaching school…After all, who but a teacher knows how important it is to raise your children with love and understanding, giving all the attention needed to mold the children and set them on the right path. Sherwood and I decided that whatever it took, we would make it our plan to keep me home with the girls while he worked. Our mortgage payment was $106 per month. If we had to sell the house, we would tighten our belts and sacrifice for our children.

We managed very well, and our lives were filled with adventure. We traveled, we explored, and life was picture perfect. "100 – 100" was still our motto and respect for each other's feelings was of utmost importance.

I slowly learned that there was nothing that Sherwood would not do for his wife or his children...or for anyone else!

Often he got a call from a friend or neighbor in need of a handyman, Sherwood would go to help. When I complained to him that I missed him being at home because he was helping people all the time, he replied: "This is who I am, would you have me not help someone in need?"

I learned slowly that his judgment was almost always right! He was kind, giving and respectful towards his family and to his friends.

When I think of the glue that has held us together all these years, I would probably say the most important thing was respect. Neither of us would ever say a harmful thing to the other, and we always consider the other in our daily thoughts and actions. I am very proud that Carrie and Andrea both acquired these traits, thoughtfulness and respect in interaction with people.

Our little Cape Cod house was beginning to get a little cramped. So Sherwood undertook the job of expanding it. With his "golden hands" he added a den, a dining room and enlarged our bedroom. We still live in the same charming home that attracted us 52 years ago.

When our daughters were in high school, I decided I would go back to work to enrich my life. The teaching field was in an uproar and it no longer looked inviting to me.

Sherwood suggested I zero in on something I loved and pursue it, rather than be a slave to a 9 to 5 job. As usual, his suggestion was perfect. I always loved travel...We would take the girls traveling to Europe during the summers, rather than send them to Summer camp. It became a learning experience for all of us. We would research the country we were to visit and map out our itinerary. Imagine Carrie's excitement when she returned to her fifth grade class after a summer spent in Greece and Rome, studying architecture, with pictures of herself by an ionic column near the Parthenon!

This love of travel led to my second career. I became a tour operator, taking groups on planned tours. At first we visited museums, Broadway shows, gardens and other places of interest in the tri-state area. Then, I planned travel to cities throughout the United States, Europe and South America. I was doing what I loved. Sherwood would arrange his generous vacation time to coincide with my trips and we were fulfilling dreams.

At age 60, Sherwood retired, with the sole purpose of helping me with my business. He was my sounding board, and guided me through significant business decisions. He helped escort extended trips and held the hands of those in need of special attention. My clients loved him. He had a special talent for anticipating a client's needs, offering a kind word or a warm gesture. I think my success as a tour operator is directly related to Sherwood. Teamwork came naturally to us.

Our relationship grew and was enriched by our many friends. Sherwood still has friends with whom he played stickball as a kid. I have wonderful friends from college days. But our very best friends are the ones we made together as a couple, friends who share our love of theater, ballet, and sightseeing. These wonderful people are the individuals we could call on when in need, those who would be there for us to bolster us in good times or bad.

Our family ties enriched our relationship. Our respective parents loved each other and would often socialize. Sherwood's late sister eventually accepted me into the family...She had doubts at first, which I attributed to the fact that she loved him and would find any woman a threat. My brother and sister-in-law were not only relatives, but were good friends as well, as they still are. Sherwood's six nieces and nephews, and my six nieces and nephews and all their children are always included in our family celebrations and holiday parties. We are definitely enriched by these get-togethers, and our children feel this way too.

In addition, our affiliation at temple was very fulfilling and afforded us many good friends. One of them recognized in Sherwood a potentially good business partner. A partnership ensued, which lasted for the next twenty five years.

Sherwood, a supervisor for an electrical company, was extremely well liked at work, and was fulfilled in his dealings with workers and his bosses. Here too, he was extremely careful in what he said…never wanting to hurt feelings. He always expressed the feeling that you gain respect by giving respect, and so he practiced this motto.

Our philosophy of "100-100" still stands. I will do anything in my power to make his life comfortable. I am sure he would do even more than that for me.

THE SECRET TO SALLIE AND SHERWOOD'S MARRIAGE?

THE POWER OF RESPECT

At first glance, Sallie and Sherwood's blind date seemed to be a recipe for disaster :"It was a hot Saturday night in July, the kind where whatever you put on sticks to you, because your body is covered with a sheen of perspiration that just won't disappear. Reluctantly, I was getting ready for yet another blind date. They all seem to be so boring, or worse, obnoxious...Sherwood showed up on time, looked okay, except for those brown wing-tipped shoes!

Brown shoes, on a first date, can you imagine?...Fortunately, Sallie was smart and soon discovered that Sherwood was "sweet, generous and, most importantly, respectful". Indeed, she quickly recognized that " he was kind, giving and respectful towards his family and to his friends...Respect for each other's feelings was of the utmost importance".

"At our wedding reception, we received a precious bit of advice from a dear friend. "Most people think marriage is a "50 – 50" deal, but it's really "100 – 100", each of you giving all to the other. The magic formula worked. "100 – 100" has been our motto throughout our married life, and to this day we still give completely to each other."

And they did have to give each other 100% of their attention. As they approached maturity, both Sherwood and Sallie were still seeking the perfect career: "Sherwood suggested I zero in on something I loved and pursue it, rather than be a slave to a 9 to 5 job. I became a tour operator, taking groups on planned tours. At first we visited museums, Broadway shows, gardens and other places of interest in the tri-state area. Then, I planned travel to cities throughout the United States, Europe and South America. I was doing what I loved. At age 60, Sherwood retired, with the sole purpose of helping me with my business...My clients loved him ... He always expressed the feeling that you gain respect by giving respect...Teamwork came naturally to us."

There are not too many qualities on this earth which are universally recognized and praised as an essential ingredient to happiness and fulfillment. Respect is one these ingredients. "I could never love where I could not respect" said Charlotte Elizabeth Aisse .

"When I think of the glue that has held us together all these years, I would probably say the most important thing was respect. Neither of us would ever say a harmful thing to the other, and we always consider the other in our daily thoughts and actions."

Sherwood and Sallie have respected each other wishes and long-term goals. They are at peace and very much in love with each other.

CHAPTER VII

Harvey and Phyllis (55 years)

"55 Years and Growing"
By Harvey and Phyllis Granat

It's hard to believe that we've lasted this long: *I am such a reserved and private person, while Harvey is very outgoing and, probably, as public as you are likely to see.*

I am an adventuress and love to travel, regardless of the distance or condition. I don't love to fly and usually like to keep our travel less than 6 hours of flying time and that's with the help of a valium.

I am a very picky eater…basics are my preference. *When we go to a dinner party, I will call ahead to make sure the hostess knows that he won't eat certain foods.* She, on the other hand, other than shell fish and pork products will try, and usually eat, anything.

I have no sense of direction, while hers is rarely fallible, and until the advent of the GPS, have been totally reliant on her whenever we leave the neighborhood.

*I can fall asleep when my head hits the pillow. Sleep and Harvey are not friends…*I read, do crossword puzzles or watch TV to get ready for sleep; all bona fide disturbances to Phyllis in bed.

When we do get into bed, I am always cold and she is usually hot and I am talking about the room temperature.

And yet, on my most recent Valentine's Day card to her, I said: "You're the half that makes me whole." Forget the "behind every great man…." theory. It is who is BESIDE every man, great or small. That is how marriage and partnership is defined.

We had both grown up in the 50's; a very unique time that influenced our lives. We knew peace, prosperity and innocence. We had parents who adored each other. There was no rock and roll, Beatles, Vietnam, drugs, birth control or Women's Movement; we were truly the white bread and loafers' generation.

From an early age I was always a little independent. I was the first person in my family to go to college; no less one "out of town" I had always wanted to be a journalist, having been an editor on the Fire Island Weekly and my high school newspaper. It was freeing, frightening and exciting to be on my own for the first time. In all my life I had never had a room of my own;

it was always shared. If you have read Anne Morrow Lindbergh's "Gifts from the Sea" you will understand this feeling.

It all began 58 years ago at the start of our freshman year at Syracuse University. One night I wandered into one of the women's dorms, at Syracuse University, with two friends of mine and I was transfixed when I saw her. There was something special that made her stand out from the room full of girls. I wish she had felt the same about me.

Her diary, which she showed me some years later, said: *"I met these 3 guys tonight; one guy was very handsome, tall and lean; another was an absolute dream; and Harvey was heavy set and very funny.* Well, guess who got the last laugh.

We went together for 4 years- we literally grew up together, sharing so many wonderful experiences. *So many of my skills, like leadership, organization and inquisitiveness were developed during my years at Syracuse.*

We married 3 weeks after graduation and 6 weeks before I went into the Army. We were very young, but certainly mature in relation to today's young people. And, so, began a journey with, bumps along the way, with a woman whom I love more today than ever.

That didn't happen with just the passage of time. It came with challenges of life and the ability to navigate those challenges through compromise and understanding, *and giving each other the space to grow, while supporting each other in our respective goals.*

However, our early years were punctuated by a recurring disagreement on the "balance of power" in the marriage. We both came from the traditional background where our fathers were the dominant of the two parents and commanded the extra respect of the spouse.

From the first days of our relationship, I wanted an equal relationship and made it very clear that we were on pedestals of equal height. It was a battle I fought throughout the first 10-12 years of our marriage and ultimately won. How interesting that "winning" turned into a victory for both of us, since having a strong partner, with an equal say, has meant the difference in our succeeding as a couple; and probably saved our marriage.

I married a strong, intelligent woman who never would have been happy in an unequal partnership.

The very first challenge I can remember was our honeymoon. From an early age, I had an intense interest in show business and the singers of the day: Como, Sinatra, Damone and, especially, Bing Crosby. I had seen every movie and owned so many of his records

So, what does this have to do with our honeymoon? I was determined to get to Hollywood and meet Bing Crosby. I tried everything and by the start of the second week, one night at the Beverly Hills Hotel, I saw Phyllis sitting at the desk, in our hotel room, and drafting a telegram to her mother that basically said: *"All he wanted was to marry me so that he could come out here and meet Bing Crosby. I don't know if this marriage is going to work."*

I stopped the telegram before it went out and, believe it or not, the next day, which was my birthday, I found out where he lived and we drove through his open security gates, I rang the bell, and before I knew it, there we were chatting away with Crosby, who could not have been nicer. Obviously, the rest of the honeymoon was a big success.

This was an early example of his setting his sights on something and not letting go until he achieved it.

COMPROMISES

One of the serious compromises was my career. I was born with a musical talent that had developed over the years to a professional level. I had years of training, and sang at every opportunity I could find, whether through high school and college shows, a regular weekly appearance on a variety show on an NBC affiliate , entertaining in hospitals when I was in service, or, really, anyplace that had an audience who would listen. I really wanted to make a career of it. But, there was a disconnect.

I wanted a normal family life which does not go with being a successful entertainer and certainly didn't go with my wife to be or her very traditional family. So, my passion was set aside...but only for 48 years; more about that later.

We started out in a small apartment in Queens with me teaching and Harvey with the thread of an idea for a new business. My dreams of becoming a journalist were totally unrealistic as women could never get a job, so teaching was the profession of the time.

There was very little money coming in and it became apparent to me that I had married someone who cared little for material possessions and cared far more about family, health and traditions.

My business idea was to create a company that would provide financing to businesses that wanted to acquire machinery and equipment and didn't have the necessary capital. My father in law was in the store fixture business, at the time. I took all of my savings, and he invested with me, and we started a company specializing in financing of fixtures and equipment for retailers.

I shared a 10 x 12 office with a kosher caterer. There was a half wall between us. I was making cold calls to retailers and he was selling cold cuts to parents of brides to be or bar mitzvah boys.

Harvey and I discussed a plan to get the company known. I suggested that he contact the editors of all the retail publications and "sell" the idea of this new financing phenomenon. He did and it worked...soon there were feature stories in all of the major trade papers and the telephone started ringing and the calendar filled up with appointments.

It didn't take very long until store fixtures expanded to office equipment and to computers and machinery. Over a period of a few years I soon had a company with branch offices in key U.S. cities and a need for substantial capital.

We found a couple of underwriters interested in taking us public and, before I knew it, we had a successful public offering with plenty of press to go along with it.

While all this was going on we started our family. I gave up my teaching position to raise the children and to help with the business, playing an important role in all the public relations and advertising that needed to be handled...brochures, press releases, interviews, internal newsletters and on and on.

The company continued to grow and we became a listed company on a major exchange. . The leasing industry, by this time, had attracted other players, both public and private and the public companies were all part of a "hot" market. The temptation to change lifestyle, and believe my own press, was very tempting. Phyllis was the bedrock of reality and never allowed us to forget the values for which we stood and which were the most meaningful to us and our family.

We opened offices abroad and she made most of the trips with me. Our management, and hundreds of employees, knew her and respected her and her role in my life. Whether it was business entertaining at The Four Seasons in New York or a private bankers' dinner at Brown's Hotel in London, I knew I could depend on her for her total support in whatever capacity needed.

WHAT ABOUT ME?

As our youngest child was soon to enter kindergarten, I began to once again have yearnings for a career of my own. I loved the law and Hofstra University was just starting its law school. Unfortunately it was not to be. Harvey and my family were all against it.

We had to confront a major issue. There came a point where Phyllis wanted to go to law school and become an attorney. The kids were young and needed their mother and, I guess, I became the roadblock to her doing this at that time. It would not be honest to say that this did not cause problems between us. It did. In no small measure it was revisiting the issue of my pursuing a career as an entertainer. Knowing our lifestyle and pressure quotients, I felt strongly about it.

As a compromise I enrolled in a Paralegal program, a new career that was in its infancy, which had much less time demands. I was the first person in our circle of friends to break out of the traditional role of homemaker and explore new options. You have to remember this was the 60's and women's rights were just in their beginnings.

She did pursue paralegal studies which enabled her to spend more limited, but nonetheless fulfilling, time in the law profession.

I never practiced as a paralegal, but instead was hired by the company that managed all the paralegal courses around the country. I became their first marketing person, and also developed the internships programs that are today such an important part of the program. I was working in the city and balancing many roles.

I never considered myself a women's liber, but I definitely felt women had equal rights.

I had put off entertaining long enough when I met a wonderful actor, Michael Moriarity. Michael had a theater company and school. They were performing Shakespeare in modern speech and I became fascinated by it. I was invited to serve on his Board and, ultimately, became Chairman, bringing others with me and raising quite a bit of money to ensure its continuity,

One day, after a Board meeting, Michael asked me an unusual question. He said: "Do you have an unfulfilled dream that I can help you to realize?" He did not know that I sang and I told him to go to the piano and play "Time After Time" in the key of C. He didn't believe what he heard and right then and there, said he wanted to produce a supper club act for me and get me some first class bookings.

This he did and I appeared at several leading clubs in the City over a period of a couple of years. Then came a period of involvement in some new business opportunities that took most of my time and it was not until some years later that something interesting happened.

We were vacationing, about 8 years ago at Rancho LaPuerta, a luxury fitness/vacation resort in Mexico where they had a sing-along one night. He is incapable of singing quietly and the next thing I knew he was standing up and performing for the guests and telling stories about the composers whose songs he sang.

My knowledge of those composers came from a hobby of many years…collecting original letters and manuscripts of the greats of the American Popular Songbook: Gershwin, Porter, Rodgers, Berlin, etc. It's quite a collection and is highlighted by the original manuscript of one of Gershwin's very well-known songs.

Management of the resort asked if he would like to come back the following year as a presenter. He readily agreed and has been doing programs there every year since. But, on the plane trip back to New York, it was I who said to him: "If you can do it there, why not contact Canyon Ranch and see if they would be interested". Canyon Ranch is the foremost spa/luxury resort in the country with locations in Lenox, Mass and Tucson, Arizona.

Well, I did and the rest is history. I have done over 150 shows there these past six years and, along the way, have made a number of appearances at Feinstein's at the Regency, Birdland, Mandarin Oriental Hotel and a host of other venues in the Northeast. There are no words to adequately express the feeling I have when I am performing before a packed room and the audience is expressing its appreciation for what I do.

It's so interesting as I look back on it. Early in our marriage, Phyllis knew nothing about show business and had very little appreciation for my passion. Today, she is as knowledgeable as anyone I know on every facet of show business and, in every way, is my partner in the planning and execution of, what has become, a very active performing career. and I am a professional entertainer, living out my life's delayed dream.

I have also been teaching "The History of The Great American Songbook" at a major university. And all of this has been with the encouragement and input of my best friend and toughest critic, Phyllis.

My interests have always been very varied and so I have zigged and zagged through many different careers and opportunities unlike so many women of my generation. I am proud that I was ahead of the curve and carved out a path for myself, and led many other women along with me. I started Career Awareness seminars in the 70's and while Harvey didn't always agree with what I was doing, he was supportive and was always there for me as a sounding board.

CORO Foundation Public Affairs Fellowship

Starting with a Public Affairs Fellowship I was awarded in the 70's, with the CORO Foundation, I have always been interested in Consumer issues.

Today I am a Mediator, having built on my years of experience with the NY State Attorney General's Office, Bureau of Consumer Fraud and Protection.

DEALING WITH CRISES

Over the years we have had to deal with some serious family issues, ranging from health to a child's very difficult marital issues to being a victim of the Madoff Ponzi Scheme; all of which were challenging to say the least. In the latter case, our long term retirement plans had to be put on hold and adjustments had to be made in our standard of living.

This was a big problem to me, but not so to Phyllis. She eliminated so much of my angst by her level-headed no nonsense approach to "the basics" of our lives and those things that were most important to us as a couple I gained even more love and respect for her

as my partner in this crisis.

YOUNG PRESIDENTS ORGANIZATION (YPO)

YPO has been one of those things that have made us grow as a couple. This international organization is comprised of members who are Presidents of companies of a minimum size, and has chapters in major cities throughout the world. We have regular meetings with some of the most interesting speakers and participants to whom one might have access.

YPO has played a major role for me, enabling me to have experiences few people are fortunate to experience. Women always had equal say, and my education from the many resources, we were exposed to, helped me grow and become more confident and comfortable with talking to anyone, be they a business leader, celebrity, entertainer or government official.

YPO has been responsible for a number of highlights of our experiences as a couple. We stood at the fence with astronaut, Pete Conrad, at Cape Canaveral as the Apollo Soyuz spacecraft lifted. As the countdown went from 5 to 4 to 3 to 2 to 1, he burst into tears and held onto Phyllis as he relived his experiences on Apollo 12.

We engaged in private conversation with President Gerald Ford, at the White House discussing the economy and went one on one with President Clinton in New York, discussing small business issues and challenges.

We hosted dozens of the biggest names in the performing arts in a series of seminars that we co-chaired.

In each of these undertakings, as partners we created some wonderful memories and took the ordinary and made it extraordinary utilizing each of our individual skills.

FAMILY TOGETHERNESS

On the occasion of the 50th Anniversary of our respective parents, we planned a very special trip with them and our children, traveling up and down the California coast. One of the highlights of the trip was a private reception with San Francisco's then Mayor and now Senator, Dianne Feinstein. She responded to a letter I had written telling her that we were celebrating this very special family event in her city.

Our three children, their spouses and our eight grandchildren are each uniquely special in their own way. But there is a common love of family that tightly links us all

We try to regularly vacation with all of our children and grandchildren. This has resulted in not only wonderful memories, but a bonding between the eight cousins that give us both great joy. *We both agree that being with our family is the most important thing to us.*

WHY I DECIDED TO LEAVE HARVEY (only temporarily)

Travel and adventure are very important to me. While Harvey likes to travel, he usually puts restrictions on where and how far we will fly. SO...I asserted my independence and have made several trips without him, but with his support.

My most recent trip was to Peru, highlighted by a visit to Macchu Picchu. I am very comfortable being alone and have always met such interesting people. My solo travel is foreign to our kids, but I think they know that there is a streak of adventure in their mother that needs to be fulfilled.

MUTUAL SUPPORT

The common threads in our marriage have been mutual respect and compromise. A marriage cannot succeed without these and we hope that we have created a model for our children and grandchildren to follow.

We have always tried to stay on the same page or, at the very least, to fully discuss and reconcile things, so that, in the end, we would be on the same page. Respecting our different points of view has strengthened our marriage and enabled each of us to grow, while maintaining a unified voice on major issues

Our home in the Berkshires is our great equalizer. When we have major problems, we try to deal with them there, where we are surrounded by the beauty and tranquility of the area. Do we solve them all? Of course not. But we can rationally discuss them and try very hard to decompress after facing them. Phyllis always has had malapropos and has said that the Berkshires allow her to "decompose". G_d, I hope not.

Like anything else in life, you need to continually work at a marriage for it to succeed. Sometimes it is hard; sometimes it is painful; but the net result can be a beautifully enduring love that becomes the umbrella of happiness under which you can handle life's exigencies.

We have been blessed to be a four generation family for as long as I can remember and it is a joy to the youngest generation instilled with the same values as we cherish. The children and grandchildren have a very special bond with Harvey's mother who, as I write this, will be celebrating her 96th Birthday and keeps in touch with every one of them on a regular basis.

WHAT HAVE 55 YEARS TAUGHT US

There has to be sharing, closeness, laughing- excitement in doing things together- feeling proud of each other- giving space to pursue individual desires.

Love is security- knowing your spouse is ALWAYS there for you- in the good times and bad.

Love is a source of strength.

Love and marriage is having your husband as partner, best friend, lover and the best role model in the world for your children and grandchildren (and maybe, one day, great grandchildren).

THE SECRET TO PHYLLIS and HARVEY's MARRIAGE?

FAMILY TOGETHERNESS

Truly, it is quite surprising that Phyllis and Harvey are still married to each other. After all, they almost divorced on their honeymoon! Phyllis, the reserved and private person in the couple, yet always ready to travel far and away on a whim, and Harvey, as outgoing as they come, who cannot get on a plane without anxiety... No wonder their marriage would encounter "bumps along the way..." In their own families, the father figure was the traditional dominant of the two parents and commanded the respect of the spouse. Harvey was quite happy with this model, but Phyllis had other views: "From the first days of our relationship, I wanted an equal relationship and made it very clear that we were on pedestals of equal height. It was a battle I fought throughout the first 10-12 years of our marriage and ultimately won."

However, Phyllis and Harvey soon discovered that, despite all their differences, they shared a strong and powerful goal: they wanted a normal family life. That common goal superseded all other individual aspirations, whether it be becoming a successful entertainer (which Harvey patiently waited for almost half a century to achieve...), or going to law school to become an attorney (which Phyllis abandoned to devote her time to raising her family, and assisting her husband in his new business)

The secret to Phyllis and Harvey's marriage is indeed family togetherness. They are the fortunate parents of three children, and vacation frequently with them, their spouses and eight grandchildren. Over the years, they have faced serious family issues, health problems, and marital as well as financial crises. But they remember the bond that unites them: "We have been blessed to be a four generation family for as long as I can remember and it is a joy to the youngest generation instilled with the same values as we cherish. The children and grandchildren have a very special bond with Harvey's mother who, as I write this, will be celebrating her 96th Birthday and keeps in touch with every one of them on a regular basis.

We both agree that being with our family is the most important thing to us: the common threads in our marriage have been mutual respect and compromise. A marriage cannot succeed without these and we hope that we have created a model for our children and grandchildren to follow."

CHAPTER VIII

Grace and Leonard (54 years)

"Love Letters and Much More:
Grace and Leonard Louis, Their Journey"
By Grace Louis

1946–2000

"When ink joins with pen, then the blank paper can say something."

—Rumi

The Songs of Love

"In my arms, in my arms am I ever gonna get that girl in my arms," was Lenny's favorite melody from the get go, which quickly turned into "our love is here to stay" once he jumped that first hurdle. Our love and affection was always there even during rough times, and we had ours, like most couples do. Our ability to talk freely and share feelings, hopes, and anxieties was a big plus. His sense of humor kept us going lots of times. I was the serious one. He was the responsible family man and husband who made me feel loved and respected.

How we met and when and where we met is what follows. My road and his path were so different! Yet we joined together in a relationship that turned into 54 and a half years of marriage until he passed away on December 9, 2000. We both took very seriously our commitment to one another and the family we created. One son and then one daughter. His essence is always with me. He was special.

Two Haiku

I learned early on
To ask for what I needed.
My wish—His Command.
A match meant to be.
It lasted half a century
'Til death us did part.

Grace's Journey: First Impressions

In my senior year of high school, my commercial law teacher and guardian angel, Mr. Tanenbaum, offered me the opportunity of a paid summer job. I would be acting as an assistant bookkeeper, also doing general clerical work as needs arose. I was 17 years old that July of 1943. The job offered good hands-on experience for a kid who was being pushed out into the real workforce after one more semester at Evander Childs High School, and then graduation. My family's needs came before my personal desire to continue my education. My dad was ill. The location of my summer employment would be the Workmen's Circle Camp in Hopewell Junction, New York. Room and board would be included.

My parents had to approve of the deal before I could move ahead with the plan. My mom insisted that she meet this teacher before sign-ing off on anything. Mr. Tanenbaum agreed to visit our apartment and assured her of his honest intent. I knew he was married and had two young children! He needed a good assistant and was certain that I was capable of doing that which would be required. Hooray! I was on my way! It was also an "away from home for the first time" job.

I was on duty during Mr. Tanenbaum's lunch break when a bus arrived earlier than expected, with two young men who had made their reservations in advance. Their rooms had been assigned and their keys were in place. All I needed to do was have them fill out the required forms for our files. I greeted them and let them know that if they filled out the forms quickly, they could still grab lunch. They said the bus had made a lunch stop so they were in no hurry.

These two young men, who I assumed were friends, were much more mature than the waiters and busboys I had met at mealtimes. Most of them were recent high school graduates. A few had finished a year of college. All were there for the big tips they could earn over the summer. Too many of them reminded me of my bratty kid brother.

I tried to engage the new arrivals in conversation while waiting for someone to show up and direct them to their quarters. Nat Lipschitz was the first to hand me the completed registration card. I noted that he lived in the Bronx. When I said I lived in the Bronx too, he thought I was flirting, because the next thing I knew he pulled out a photo of his girlfriend and said he was engaged. I admired her photo and wished him well.

Then I picked up Leonard Louis's card. I teased him about his two first names. I told him my father's first name was Louis. He had an engaging smile. But what I liked most were his eyes. The color, hard to describe, was sort of a speckled khaki green. In spite of the glasses he wore, his gaze was most amazing. He wasn't that tall (5'9"), but he wasn't too short, either. I just sensed that this young man was worth getting to know better. I was so right.

What follows is Leonard's personal journey to our meeting place and his first impressions of me. He wrote down these thoughts in 1995, when we were working together on sorting out our exchange of letters. We had both saved every letter we had received from one another. They are quite a collection and they will speak for themselves.

Leonard's Journey: First Impressions

I was in my senior year at Buffalo State Teachers' College when I received notification from the Army Air Corps that my application for teaching Aircraft Mechanics had been accepted.

I set up an appointment with the dean of the Industrial Arts Department. He was positive about the opportunity and insisted that after the war I complete my degree program.

So off I went to Chanute Field in Rantoul, Illinois, and started my teaching career. After a year in Illinois, I was transferred to Goldsborough, North Carolina. After completing another year, I found that teaching the same subject was most repetitive and frankly boring.

I made a major decision! I would quit my teaching job and enlist in the military. Family and friends thought I was insane. Perhaps I was. That decision changed my life. I decided to spend a few weeks before reporting for active duty at a camp in upstate New York.

Isn't it strange how a simple decision like the choice of a resort can impact on one's life! That proved to be the best decision I had ever made. When I went to register, a young lady named Grace took care of the necessary details, and my life was changed forever. I was astonished by her beauty and her bubbly personality. I had stumbled into a fantasy, and I spent two glorious weeks working around her schedule. I tried to make the most of every minute we had together. I resented the time she had to work.

It was rough when I had to leave, but I knew I could endure the rigors of military service knowing what could be waiting for me. Something concrete and meaningful. I prayed that Grace felt the same way. I was smitten with her. With her overall appearance, her good looks, her personality. This had not happened to me before. I was determined to pursue her. And pursue her I did after I entered the Army Air Corps.

The Courtship: Letters

Len started wooing me through the mail as soon as he got home: This letter was received on July 26, 1943, at Workmen's Circle Camp. It was his first.

Monday, 11 AM

Dear Grace,

As you can plainly see, you made a most definite impression on me. Here it is approximately 24 hours since I last saw you and I find myself writing you. As I told you at camp, I am not a sentimentalist. At least I don't think I have been one up until now. But believe me, Grace, when I say that I miss you . . . As I look back in retrospect at my stay at camp, I can find only one dark cloud in the clear sky—my failure to kiss you right on those ruby red lips of yours. Let me assure you that I wanted to do this in the worst way. Especially when you were standing at the bus saying goodbye. Someday I will kiss you and you better be prepared for the surprise that will be in store for you.

Yesterday, while walking me to breakfast, you mentioned that you had lost two combs. I am therefore sending you an instrument for adjusting, cleaning and coiffing your Tesian[1]* blonde locks.

Well I must close now as I have a dental appointment.
Love, Lenny P.S. May I look forward to a reply?
July 27, 1943—

A fantasy date.

Hello Operator? Workmen's Circle Camp, Hopewell Junction, New York, please. Hello, is Grace there please? Hello honey, how are you? Fine. What are you doing tonight? Nothing? Swell. Let's go places. Will you meet me? Or shall I call for you? Okay. I'll be up in about two hours. So long.

Come on honey. Let's take a cab. Don't be silly, it's okay, I've got plenty of money. And besides the best is none too good. Hey, taxi! There, isn't that better than the nasty subway? Let's eat first. Hey driver. The Astor please. And take your time.

Boy that was some swell dinner. Now what show would you like to see? Okay, let's go. Taxi! The best show in town please. And hurry, we don't have much time. Two tickets please. In front row center. Orchestra, of course! I don't care what they cost, let me have them.

What a show. Best I've ever seen. Now let's go somewhere for a drink and a dance or two. Hey, taxi! Stork Club please. Gee honey, it's swell dancing with you. I wish this could go on forever. No, it's not the drinks. I only had one but I feel as though I've had a dozen. Gee, it's getting late. Almost two o'clock. I'd better be getting you home. But I wish we were only starting. Taxi! Burnside Avenue in the Bronx, and spare the horses. So soon?

---

1 * Len's spelling of "Titian."

Here it is. Keep the change. Oh well honey, it was lovely being with you tonight. Let's do it again soon, okay? Good night, sleep tight.

Love,

Lenny

July 29, 1943

Dear Grace,

Had a few hours to spare yesterday afternoon, and during that time I managed to turn out the following little verse. If you recall, I promised to send you a little poem when and if I was ever in the mood. Well, yesterday I was and now this:

What word is sweeter than sweetheart?

Words to describe you are few.

Of all the sweethearts

I've met in storybooks, there's not one to compare with you.

Each time that I call you sweetheart, my thoughts go searching anew

For some word sweeter than sweetheart

But sweetheart will have to do.

That is all. There is no more. And I hope it meets with your approval. So, until next time.

With love, Lenny.

Grace's Letters

I responded to each letter in my own uncertain "where was all this going" way. I wanted to continue this relationship, but I wanted it to slow down a little bit. I had to be more certain of my feelings before I would even sign off "Love, Grace" when I corresponded with him.

My responses to his letters lacked all feelings. Remember, they were written by a 17-year-old. His letters to me were all feelings. Notice how I signed off compared to Len. Only one of his letters came to me with his Bronx home return address. After that, he was officially in the Army Air Corp. It took me until September 1st to give him my home address. He wrote to me almost every day. Initially I wasn't very prolific, but that changed over time.

July 29, 1943

Dear Lenny,

I am so rushed for time, but I suppose I ought to squeeze in one or two letters so first of all to you.

Thank you for your lovely letters. Whoever told you you couldn't write? I really enjoyed that evening we imaginarily spent together and hope that someday, in the very near future, we can make it a reality. Every little detail, right down to the good night was perfect. Your poem too was just out of this world. Where and however did you think up such a monstrosity? But, seriously, it really is beautiful.

The camp is filled to capacity again for the entire week. I suppose it will be that way for the rest of the season judging from the reservations that pile in daily—darn it!

The newlyweds left for New York on Monday. They were a little peeved at your not saying good-bye. They consoled themselves saying you probably didn't think it was right to wake them up so early.

Oh! Gosh! Another bus just pulled in—back to work I must go.

Grace

August 6, 1943

Dear Lenny,

With autumn drawing near, the weather is becoming more pleasant daily. It's still pretty hot but there is such a lovely breeze. The camp is very crowded though. We have been filled to capacity since the weekend you were here.

We played 2 basketball games this week on Tuesday and Thursday and won both. Hilltop was our first victim and Camp Kiwana next. We just seem to have an undefeatable team. Secunda's usual followed each game. Outside of that, there hasn't been much doing lately.

Now that I let you in on all the news from here, how about some news from over there? Did you get the usual injections and the usual sickness that follows? Any KP yet? In other words in general what do you do to pass the time. Write a lengthy letter real soon giving me full details.

I think I'm going into the city this Sunday to stay through Monday night. My mother seems to want to see me so I might just as well be accommodating.

I must close here and get back to work before someone gets wise to me.

Grace

Home on Leave

A dramatic change in our relationship took place after we met again in person, when I was at home in December 1943. I was back in school. He was in on a furlough for two weeks before going overseas. We met every evening and weekends while he was in town. I let him kiss me and just knew there was something happening. Call it good chemistry. It felt right and good. I knew I wanted more. Len had already known what he wanted for a long time.

I was introduced to his family during that time: his parents and sister, and his brother, Nat, whom I had already met at Workmen's Circle Camp. Nat Lipschitz had not yet changed his last name (he later did) and I was clueless until then that they were sibs. Len had legally made the name change in March of 1942. Len at 25 was the youngest in his family.

I was from a family exactly the same in size, only I had an older sister and a younger brother. I was the middle child—a difficult position in a dysfunctional family like mine.

Both families had suffered enormous financial losses. My father lost his retail men's clothing business during the Depression. He never earned a decent living subsequent to that loss. I know he tried.

Len's family lost everything when a hurricane wiped out his father's new venture—a brick factory in Florida. They were not insured. His dad was floundering, too. He was a plumber by trade so he was able to support his family. He always had a scheme.

No family fortunes for us to be a part of. We knew we would be on our own, and that was okay.

The Beginning of a Long Separation

In December of 1943 Len started on his journey around the world (China, Burma, India, the Mariana Islands in the Pacific). His crossing was on a ship stripped of all luxuries. It was not a very easy crossing, since he was not a good sailor. He spent much of that trip in the infirmary. He wrote to me regularly. We grew together and closer even though we were oceans apart.

I finished High School and was granted a Commercial Diploma. I was employed as a full charge bookkeeper and secretary. I took shorthand and used it at work and at night school. I was determined to earn those few academic credits I needed (algebra and Spanish) before CCNY would admit me to their night school.

Work, school, homework, letters to Len and my kid brother in the Navy! I was in overdrive as usual. I wrote the following in 1944, and you can sense the mood:

I was 18 the next summer.
It was a bummer.

A year had gone by
Since I met my guy.

He was off fighting a war
So no knocks on my door.

The girls huddled together
Regardless of the weather.

We bowled and we swam
We moved without a plan.

Time was a heavy load
Peace our only road.

It took another year or two
For our wishes to come true.

Len Proposes

Len informally proposed to me in his letter dated 7/1/44, and again on 12/25/44. Here are some excerpts:

Saturday—July 1st 1944

Hello Honey:

Another week has rolled around and even as time progresses I still manage to think of you as often as is possible. All of my actions seem to tie in with you in some way or another, and how I love it! I look at your pictures many times during the day and really sigh every time I do so. You seem to have gotten under my skin dear, and I can give you fair warning now that you had better be careful when and if I return to the states. I am really going to keep you busy, in fact some fine Sunday afternoon if we don't have much to do we can even go out and get hitched. What do you think about that?

December 25, 1944

Honestly Grace, of all the girls I have known and dated, there has never been one like you. To me you incorporate all the things I desire in a woman, and I want you to know that. I care for you more than anyone I know. There is something about you I can't resist—and when I get your letters I feel mighty proud and happy. The way I feel now, I would only be too glad to make you my wife, but in all fairness to both of us, we must wait until I return so we can pick up where we left off.

Our Life as a Couple Begins

Len had entered the service as a buck private and was discharged as a Sgt. Major. The highest non-commissioned rank! He had turned down the

OCS offer. It would have kept him in service for years longer. He was not interested in rank. He wanted out. He was discharged from the Army Air Corps in December of 1945. I got the following telegram from him when he returned to the United States after a 21-day trip across the Pacific:

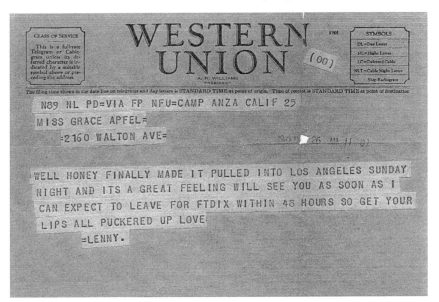

Len formally proposed to me in early spring 1946. He took me on that fantasy date and I said "Yes!" Then our lives together really took off.

We were both working that spring of 1946 and were planning a honeymoon for that summer. Len was able to purchase a gem of a used car from a friend. Instead of trading it in, he sold it to us for a song. It was our first car, a dark-green four-door LaSalle.

On July 20, 1946, we married and did indeed take off on our honeymoon trip: Washington, DC, (my choice) and Niagara Falls (his choice). He wanted me to see where he had gone to school at Buffalo State Teachers' College and to view Niagara Falls. We were all over the place. But who cared. We were together.

We opened joint checking and savings accounts as soon as we were married. There was absolute trust where money was concerned. I was not going to walk in my mother's footsteps and have to ask for what I wanted or needed. Everything went smoothly for a while. Then, one month when I went to do a bank reconciliation statement, I encountered problems. Len had neglected to record the stubs for a few checks he had drawn. We had a long talk about how to deal properly with the checkbook—stub first, check next. Remember I was a full charge bookkeeper. I could do a profit and loss statement for a business. A bank reconciliation statement was usually a lark. He pleaded with me to take charge of the checkbook since it came so easily to me. I would pay all the bills and then I would reconcile the bank statement, avoiding angst each month. It worked for us.

This dealing with personal household finances stood me in good stead when Len passed away. One of my friends, who never handled a checkbook, didn't know where to start when her spouse died. Len was not an "always must be in charge of the money" man. Len was my kind of man. It was our money, and most of the time he was the only breadwinner. We had been searching for an apartment in the Bronx, to be near both families, with no success. The failure of the New York City planners to include affordable housing for returning service men and their families was the first big bump in our road. As a result, in order to have our privacy, we rented a room in a small residential hotel. We had our own bathroom but we had to share a kitchen. We both worked, so it was adequate for the short run. We talked and planned for our future together. Our plans did include having a family, once we had adequate living quarters.

As the fates would have it, we found ourselves pregnant! This news was met with mixed emotions. The pregnancy was the result of faulty birth control. The condom apparently was defective. (I had not yet been fitted for a diaphragm.) Abortion was not a consideration—it was also illegal in the forties. Our family of the future was now in bold sight.

The bottom line was that we had both wanted children in our lives. This gift, this miracle of a child of our own, was quickly embraced with open hearts and minds. It was more proof of our love and affection for one another. A huge change of plans was now required.

This pregnancy pushed us into accepting my parents' offer to live with them temporarily. They did have the space because my brother was in the Navy. We had our own large bedroom. It was a tough decision accepting that offer. We really wanted and craved our own space. But how could we prepare formula in a shared kitchen that wasn't exactly clean? We compromised our needs for the child that wasn't yet born. A pattern throughout our lives.

Before we moved in, I felt compelled to set ground rules with my Mom about who would be handling this child. I was very serious about my parenting role and wanted to do things my way. I was reading books and talking to friends who recently had children. I was determined to be well prepared. There are three books I remember reading that I learned so much from. I still own these books:

The Rights of Infants, by Margaret A. Ribble, MD
The Happy Family, by John Levy, MD, and Ruth Munroe, PhD
Baby and Child Care, by Benjamin Spock, MD

I was seven months into our pregnancy when we made the move to live with my parents. Two weeks into my eighth month, I woke up with Malaria-type uncontrollable chills and a very high fever. I was delirious. I had seen my doctor the week before and everything had checked out. The doctor was called, Len was called, and an ambulance was called, which took me to University Heights Hospital where my doctor would meet us. Tests determined I had a severe infection. Doctor Reisman said there was a new drug on the market, streptomycin, that he thought would be effective. However, he wasn't certain it would not adversely affect the fetus. Len decided that, since my life was at stake, they had to take a chance with this new drug. If the fetus was affected, we would handle it.

Thankfully, both the fetus and I came through that ordeal. Our son was born with everything in place. He was healthy and normal, and so was

I. We were forced to sell our car to help pay all the extra medical bills. Three years later, when our daughter was born, we had no medical problems.

Len's Family

Without discussion, Len's father had planned for Len to go into the family retail hardware business when he returned from service. It was a risky scheme to begin with. Instead, Len took a job at the Veterans Administration, in the capacity of Training Officer, to support his new family. With a child in the picture, he needed a guaranteed income. Unfortunately, Len's decision to put our growing family first was not well received. My entering the picture spoiled his parents' scheme for him, and they never did let us forget it. They were mean-spirited people. His brother, Nat, the "good" boy, chose to work with his father. Nat's wife was employed and no children were on their way. It was a risk they could better afford. The business failed in a few years.

> "Stamp of approval
> That's what I kept hoping for
> I never got it."

In the background of all our joy there was also the knowledge that Len's sister, who had married during the war, was unable to conceive a child. Len's brother and his wife, who also married while Len was in the service, were also having difficulty conceiving. His sister adopted a child years later. His brother and his wife eventually had two daughters. Their third child died shortly after birth. Faced with an unplanned fourth pregnancy, they chose abortion. This was in the sixties, and under normal circumstances abortion was still illegal, so she feigned a nervous breakdown in order to receive a medically approved abortion.

Moving On

Like a dream, when our son was nine months old, a large studio apartment in Manhattan came our way. The landlord let us take over the space with a short-term lease. We were joyous! This was actually the third move we made in the first year of our marriage. We just took it all in stride. And besides, Len would now be able to walk to his job at the Veterans Administration. He came home for lunch frequently.

On Our Own: Haiku

We loved our new space
And continued to thrive there
It was a smart move.

Len washed the dishes
And changed our baby's diapers.
Love was all around.

I encouraged him
To get that college degree
With his name on it

Choice was NYU.
So under the GI Bill
That promise fulfilled.

I typed his papers
So I always felt involved
And I learned so much.

I just knew someday
It would become my turn
Choice—to wait for now.

Len's job at the VA provided earnings adequate to support us. Together we had planned on my being a stay-at-home mom. I made new friends in Manhattan, with other moms who had young children. We met in Madison Square Park, which was in walking distance from our apartment. There were three families involved. Our husbands all got along. Our children, all boys, were all within a few months of one another in age. We were all in smaller-than-desired living quarters. We all wanted second children. Lots of dialogue about where do we go from here.

Levittown was being built at that time but it was a bit far for us. A lot of affordable housing was going up in Queens. We traveled to Queens with one of the couples who owned a car, to search for larger space. We had been living in Manhattan for over two years by the time we became pregnant again, by choice. We were thrilled and did rent a larger apartment in Queens, which was supposed to be ready for occupancy a month before my due date.

1950 was a year full of happenings! Of course our new apartment was not ready when we were told it would be. We added a tiny crib to our small apartment, but who cared. Our baby girl was well and a beauty. We moved a few months later than expected.

My kid brother married two weeks after our baby was born. I was able to attend the wedding. I found a dress in my closet that actually fit my after-childbirth figure. Two weeks after the wedding, the newlyweds took off to Hollywood, California, to follow his dream. My sister had married in 1949 and now lived in Montreal, Canada. They were expecting their first child before the year 1950 was out. My Mom and Dad were adjusting to an empty nest. The three children they had brought into the world were all married. In September 1950 my father died of a massive heart attack.

My Mom was really sad and frightened, and would now be home all alone. Our new small apartment in Queens, which we had only recently moved into in the spring of 1950, became her haven. When she started talking about giving up her apartment in the Bronx and moving in with us, I felt compelled to steer her in another direction. I can still hear myself making this proposal: "We need our space, and you need and can have your own. Move to a smaller apartment, one you can better afford and visit us whenever you want. Living together would not be feasible for me. If you need to get a job, look for one in which you can utilize those unusual skills which you already have."

My mother was an experienced hair weaver. She began working in her field shortly thereafter and kept that same job until she retired. She was only 50-something when my father died. She was a skilled and responsible worker. She also relocated to a smaller apartment in the Bronx neighborhood that was familiar to her. She took the subway to work.

She never did make new friends or take the time for her own socialization needs. So I ended up having to raise a third person, my Mom. In an attempt to keep her fears and superstitions at bay and away from my kids, I introduced her to new ways of dealing with children. It was a challenge! We all gave her love and affection, and she gave us hers in return. My kids adored her. Life as a family was never the same after 1950. With my siblings out of the picture, I had become an only child. But I had a tremendously supportive spouse who understood my mother's needs.

Len commuted to Manhattan via bus and subway for a while. This was quite a change from walking to work, but he did this graciously for his family's benefit.

We bought our first new car during those years in Alley Pond Garden Apartments. I learned to drive. He taught me and taught me well. I got my license on my first try. Len looked for and got a job in Nassau County. That was a big step up from the VA. He then worked for the Naval Training Device Center in Port Washington. I again encouraged him to go back for his master's degree. Each degree offered better job opportunities with higher pay. He earned his MPA in 1959.

Sharing Experiences: Changes, Challenges and Triumphs

We moved to a three-bedroom co-op in Little Neck, Queens, and remained there for almost 40 years. We finally had bedrooms for each child. The children became of school age and I had assumed I would be able to get a job or go to school myself.

But those city planners did not factor in schools for the new community. The Board of Education had to "double-session" the one elementary school in the area. One child went to school from eight to twelve, the other from twelve to four. There was no way I was going to be home for one child and not the other.

I became an activist in the community. A group of us took a local census and proved our need for an additional elementary, junior high, and high school. By the time they were all built it was too late for my children to benefit from a normal school schedule. But the community at large was in much better shape.

I was also one of the founding members of the Samuel Field YMYWHA and sat on its Board of Directors for almost 40 years. Up until that point, after-school activities and social services were just not available locally. Determination and hard work brought that project from a dream to a reality with the help from the philanthropist Mr. Samuel Field. We got our building.

Len volunteered at the Credit Union of the Naval Training Device Center. He bowled with his buddies. We always had "things" going on separately as well as together and we shared our experiences.

I was always taking courses, one at a time, at the local colleges. I was collecting credits toward my never-forgotten goal. I also took a course offered at the Y in Folk Guitar and had a real flair for the instrument. I had a pleasant singing voice and I knew lots of songs, a perfect combination. I had been in the glee club all through elementary and high school. With an eye toward earning a few dollars, I decided I would perform at children's parties. A friend created costumes, and with my guitar and a bag of small percussion instruments I was off and running: "Travel Along in Song with Grace and Her Guitar." The Yusen's party goods store put my brochure into the hands of their customers, my only means of advertising. I worked most weekends when Len was home. That fun job lasted a few years.

Len also found a creative way to bring in additional income. He and a co-worker at the Naval Training Device Center decided they would run Charter Flights to places abroad. They named their new company The Civil Service Recreation Association. I became involved in their record keeping but I didn't want to continue doing that for too long. It kept me at home bookkeeping. I needed work where I would be interacting with people.

Len retired from his job at the NTDC after 24 and a half years of civil service employment because the center was being moved to Orlando, Florida. Not a place we wanted to go to. He was already involved in a small company he had started called Research Media, Inc., and hated to leave it. Our daughter was in her senior year of high school. Our son was away in college so his input was minimal. We talked our way through the hurdles. Lenny took early retirement—an expensive decision—but our daughter was able to finish her senior year in the high school where she had started. Our decision was a great relief to her.

Len and I started working full time at Research Media. I did have the skills to manage an office and I put them to good use. I also took a certificate course at Hofstra University in "Management by Objectives" to update and learn some new skills. The computer was not yet being used by small businesses. In just a few years we built that business to where we had sales of over a million dollars. But cash flow was a serious problem. Our customers were schools, universities and colleges. They paid, but slowly. We were definitely undercapitalized. The money man was a ruthless SOB and took over control before we knew what hit us. He wanted the business to move to Massachusetts where he lived. We said no. Research Media failed under his command in less than a year. Len got a job at G.A.F. as their Audio Visual Product Manager. After a few years he switched gears again and became a commissioned salesman for an audio cassette company. When we left the Research Media venture I finally felt free to follow my dream of going for a degree. It was my turn. It was 1975 and I was 49 years old.

In 1977 I earned a BS degree from Empire State College. My major was Developmental Psychology. I earned a third of my credits from Life Experience, a third from Independent Study, and a third from courses taken at accredited universities.

In 1980, I earned my MA from New York University. In 1983 I earned a Certificate from the Workshop Institute for Living-Learning.

I started working as a parent counselor/infant toddler educator by introducing a new program, CAPE (Child And Parent Experience) at the YMCA in Flushing, New York. It was renamed MATE (Mom And Tot Experience) for Bay Terrace Center YMYWHA. I ended up opening a program called "Time to Grow" in Bayside, New York, before I retired.

Long Beach Calls

Len's health really started going downhill, but we made the retirement move to Long Beach in 1992. I must have spent about a dozen years doing "my thing" before I called it quits. It was a job I loved and I know I touched many lives in a positive way. I had Len's full support of my efforts all along. I would write papers and he would type for me. We exchanged even that favor. Our union was meant to be.

We did make six trips abroad between 1983 and 2000 in between taking care of Len's health issues. I don't think Len's spiral down, or the enduring sense of humor with which he faced it all, can be better described than by the following lists that he prepared before each visit to his physician. These notes were written on 11/7/2000, a month before he died.

> *PATIENT—Leonard LOUIS*
> > *220 W. Broadway*
> > *Apt. #203*
> > *Long Beach, NY 11561*
> > *Date of Birth—June 19th, 1918*

MEDICAL HISTORY:
- *Triple By-Pass—9/1/83—St. Francis*
- *By-Pass Surgery—11/30/92—St. Francis*
- *Heart Surgery—2/7/93—St. Mary's, Milwaukee*
- *Prostate Surgery—2/89—St. Francis—Dr. Barbaris*
- *Stay at St. Francis—Kidney Problem—January 1996*

- *Congestive Heart Failure—February 1996—St. Francis*
- *Congestive Heart Failure—March 26, 1998—Long Beach Hospital*
- *Compressed Disc Fracture—August 1999—Dr. Mauri*

Thursday November 7th, 2000
Visit to: Dr. Nicosia
Patient: Leonard LOUIS

General Comments:

- *My weight is now 135 pounds. What is happening?*
- *Do you suggest that I wear support hose? Would that be of any value? Tried it years ago without success.*
- *I need a prescription for Physical Therapy—undated!*
- *I am constantly itching! It is driving me insane. Can anything be done about eliminating this condition?*
- *Just walking is becoming more difficult. (And in addition the Mets keep losing!)*
- *I need a prescription for a controlled substance.*
- *Otherwise everything is great!*
- *Could you direct me to the "fountain of youth?" Did you take such a course while in med school?*

I was always there for him during his hospital stays, as were his adult children. We all loved him dearly. My personal high tolerance level for adversity was developed long before I got married. As a kid, my dad was sick frequently.

How We Lived and Loved in Our Long Term Relationship

Our relationship had a very solid foundation, which could not be toppled by interfering in-laws, housing problems, struggle for financial security, etc. We managed to put our children through college. They each have their master's degrees in their field of choice. Len and I shared goals and mutual love and respect for one another. Our family unit mattered much. Oh yes, we had some heated exchanges, but that came with my starting out as a black and white thinker. It was right or it was wrong!

Shades of gray came with maturity and learning to compromise in ways I thought were for the better good of our family. I learned to be more flexible in some areas. We never went to sleep not talking to one another. Len did his share of compromising as well.

The chemistry was always good. The commitment to one another was always strong. We did not take those promises (our vows) lightly. Changes bring challenges and we shared many. We both had the ability to communicate openly and honestly with one another. We had all those years of writing about our thoughts and feelings, which resulted in an easy open dialogue that lasted forever.

And we really listened—did not just hear—but truly listened to one another. Discussions were sometimes heated and lengthy. His perception of incidents and mine sometimes differed. We usually got to the core of an issue and it was worked on over time. All relationships are unique and complex and I found that in my search for happiness, my expectations were sometimes unrealistic. Should I really have expected him to take me to the ballet when he wanted to watch a Mets game; or always hit the hamper with his underwear and socks instead of the floor; or always put the toilet seat down; or always put the cap back on the toothpaste? After all, he did wash dishes and change diapers.

Anyway, according to Mark Twain, "Happiness ain't a thing in itself. It's only in contrast with something that ain't pleasant."

So, in conclusion, our love was not made of clay. Our love was here to stay.

TOAST

For Grace and Lenny's Fiftieth Anniversary
By their daughter, Helene Louis Neffson

Here we are at dinner . . . again
Celebrating five times ten.
What can we say after all these years?

Except that one thing is very clear—
fifty years is a damn long time
(and this toast will be tough to rhyme).
Lots of caring, lots of changes,
lots of love and loss at all the stages.
Yet we're ALL here together to celebrate.
We're five living proofs of your first date,
of five long decades of constant caring,
of work, play, travel, parenting and sharing.

I—The Beginning
A Workmen's Circle rendezvous,
Two city slickers knew just what to do,
in the country in the midst of war,
a romantic fling turned into more,
turned into letters across the seas,
long-distance courtship became the key
to two young hearts in different lands.
From the Bronx to India and Japan
The postman was busy for a long, long time
while each had adventures of different kinds.
Then the hero returned seeking lost dog,
lost that, but got much more than he foresaw.

II—After the War
In a jiffy, the returning vet and girl
went out on the town and fell for each other. In a whirl-
wind of courtship and a celebration of peace,
they thought their romance would never cease.
Until quite magically, Daniel came to life,
And they became parents as well as man and wife.
They made new friends in Madison Square Park,
they set up a home and must have kept the spark
because three years later Helene joined the team
and they took to the suburbs, a brand new scene.

III—The Burbs

We children grew more quickly than the LIE,
new friends for all, community work for Gracie,
a second job for Len, we moved to Little Neck
they raised us to be menches. We had a heck
of a good time on family vacations,
driving cross country to see our relations
or heading north to New Hampshire in allergy season.
Dan's bar mitzvah gave them a reason
to gather neighbors, family and friends,
to dance and celebrate their union again.

Eisenhower watched us on the grainy black and white
and Mr. Clean and Spic and Span made everything right.
Baby boom dinners, matzo balls and sedars; wrestling on the rug
playing cards or scrabble, lots of love and hugs,
picnics in Port Washington, little league games or dance
recitals (or tonsillitis)—our days were enhanced
by their preserving love and impeccable housekeeping.
They kept us all intact and dried our eyes when we were weeping
Tootsie, Geetle, Liebish, mom and dad—
The names were changing, but the love remained. Eeeh gaad!

IV—Changes

Puberty in the children brought changes;
the couple went into business and a whole new range
of new venues kept Grace and Lenny growing together.
But would the marriage weather their new business relations
at the same time as the pubescent tribulations
of their kids? They pulled it off long enough
to get us through college. Though it got tough,
they never let it knock them out—instead
Len took another job, and Grace stuck her head
in her books and came up with two diplomas and a new career.
A new phase of freedom is beginning, that is clear.

V—The Grandchildren

They take up travel and grand parenting.
They see Italy and France and Israel. They sing
praises for each patiently-awaited grandchildren.
They fly to California to meet Katie and go wild.
Then cry when Talia moves out west,
But love prevails, survives the test.
Always remembering birthdays,
Ecstatic at Julie's arrival, always willing to play
in the pool or chat, always ready with matzo balls,
turkey sandwiches, board games, and telephone calls.

VI—Long Beach

After all the scars and surgeries and Mets losses,
we're celebrating fifty years. Len still crosses
his fingers that his dusting will pass inspections,
vitamins and potions diminish her arthritis and her waistline.
Always the ocean's soothing splash.
Now there is time to watch the sunlight shift and flash
as you sit on the balcony and muse,
or head for the boardwalk and enjoy all the blues
of the ever changing sea and sky.
There is time to ponder that eternal why,
to enjoy the grandchildren as they zoom
into adolescence, waxing and waning like the moon,
to see your graying children survive middle-age forces.
To enjoy old friends and mourn others' loses,
to meet new comrades, read books and tell stories,
to let go of all the old worries.

We toast you two,
Happy Fiftieth Anniversary!
We love you!

THE SECRET TO GRACE AND LEONARD'S MARRIAGE?

THE POWER OF HUMOR

Love is the Joy of the good, the wonder of the wise,
the amazement of the Gods.

—Plato

Grace and Leonard created a world built on hope, with just the right touch of humor, which helped them through the trial and tribulations of their life together as a couple.

Soon after Leonard met Grace at a summer camp where she was employed, the recently inducted young soldier found himself leaving New York, for basic training with the Army Air Corp, in Florida.

In survival mode, to maintain her attention, he sent a letter to his brand new girlfriend, dated July 27, 1943, in which he described a fun filled, fabulous, fantasy to his new girl-friend.

Len continued to woo and court Grace through the mail. Both Len and Grace saved all the letters of their courtship… and that titillating telegram! Len was discharged from the Army Air Corp in December of 1945. They were wed on July 20, 1946. Their marriage lasted over 54 years.

They lived and loved through happiness and sadness and much playfulness. They never lost that wonderful sense of humor even when Len eventually became seriously ill… Grace wrote:" I don't think Len's spiral down, or the enduring sense of humor with which he faced it all, can be better described than by the following lists that he prepared before each visit to his physician. These notes were written on 11/7/2000, a month before he died."

Thursday November 7th, 2000
Visit to: Dr. Nicosia
Patient: Leonard LOUIS
General Comments:

- *My weight is now 135 pounds. What is happening?*
- *Do you suggest that I wear support hose? Would that be of any value? Tried it years ago without success.*
- *I need a prescription for Physical Therapy—undated!*
- *I am constantly itching! It is driving me insane. Can anything be done about eliminating this condition?*
- *Just walking is becoming more difficult. (And in addition the Mets keep losing!)*
- *I need a prescription for a controlled substance.*
- *Otherwise everything is great!*
- *Could you direct me to the "fountain of youth?" Did you take such a course while in med school?*

We all know that laughter makes us feel better. There is strong scientific data to prove us right. Even pretending to be happy, attempting a smile, will trigger positive emotions. In her superb review, "The Simulation of Smiles (SIMS) model: Embodied simulation and the meaning of facial expression" (Behavioral and Brain Sciences,Vol. 33; 6. Cambridge Univ Press, 2010), Paula M Niedenthal and her coauthors describe the science behind smiles. "In a classic study, participants were instructed to hold a felt-tip marker in their mouths in a way that caused their facial muscles to be formed into a smile or a frown. While holding the marker this way, they were asked to view comic strips and say how funny they found them. Those whose facial muscles were mimicking a smile found the same comics funnier than those whose facial muscles were set into a frown." Laughter triggers a release of endorphins and dopamine by the brain, which in turn increases the feeling of relaxation and reduces stress. People who laugh often are less likely to feel depressed, anxious or tensed. Their marriages and relationships are happier and more successful. They see life with hope and optimism.

Of course, Grace misses her companion, her life partner. But her memories are still filled with happiness and laughter. She has learned – and taught- the 4Cs of a successful marriage: Chemistry, Commitment, Communication and Compromise.

...And that, ladies and gentlemen, is what makes a great marriage!

CHAPTER IX

David and Isabel (54 years)

"From the Old World and the New
(And Everywhere in Between)"
By Isabel Taylor

Portugal

It was a June evening in 1959, at a cocktail party in an elegant estate. A handsome man approached me. In a soft voice with a very slight accent from the American South, he struck up a conversation. He was a paragon of politeness and charm. David asked someone who I was. When he heard that I was only 18, he said, "I am not here to do any baby-sitting!"

I grew up in an aristocratic world. We were four children, and during the summer had three governesses – English, French and Portuguese – so we learned three languages fluently. My father was the Count of Mangualde, Vila Real and Mello, a handsome man of honor and integrity, and an excellent engineer. He was dedicated to saving Mateus, our beautiful ancestral home in the north, where we spent our vacations. My mother was one of the great beauties of her day. She literally stopped traffic, as did her sister Maya. She was also brilliant and charming. Family and tradition were everything – our roots went back to the age of chivalry, and were planted firmly in Portuguese soil.

So how did David K Taylor, a Southern boy, from North Carolina, end up in my world that night? He was fascinating: from the New World but without the coarseness Americans were supposed to have. One of the brief facts I knew about him was that he was leading a team that was searching for oil off the coast of Portugal. An oilman, with class!

That fall, there was a fancy benefit for the Red Cross at a friend's house. Over there, tending bar, was the young man (Juanito) who would become King of Spain – and there, parking cars was the son of the King of Italy. And there... that American again! This time I got to hear him sing. With a beautiful lyric tenor voice, he sang "On the Street Where You Live", from a new musical, My Fair Lady. He had a cultured soul. After that party, we went out with a group of friends. The evening ended with an invitation to a dinner he was hosting a few days later. David had come to Portugal as an international concessions negotiator, to manage Mobil Oil's exploration affiliate there, which was in association with the Portuguese Petroleum Company and the Axel Johnson interests of Sweden.

I started learning things about this David Taylor. When he was singing "On the Street Where You Live", he wasn't singing it to me; apparently, he was pursuing a 35-year-old widow. Which made sense, for a 30-year-old successful businessman. I was just 19, a teenager.

At that dinner, there were about ten of us. He was witty, smart and cultured. He obviously also had a powerful drive: he went to college at 15 and followed it up with law school, both at Duke University. By the age of 20 he was done with all his studies, including his law degree. He seemed not the least romantic. When I said his penthouse apartment, with its endless terraces, must be beautiful when the moon was full, he said, "But then, you can see the moon from all over town!" Hmm.

It was then that we had our first disagreement: what is the difference between Honor and Honesty? He said it was the same thing: if you are honest, you are honorable. Very… Protestant. But my Catholic upbringing, steeped in etiquette and Old-World manners – had taught me differently. Pure honesty can be hurtful, and honor could demand certain attitudes that might not be honest. David, a stickler for the English language, was surprised that anyone would dare argue with him about words. I countered that it was not a question of semantics, but rather values and principles.

But apparently our disagreement had gotten his interest. I went that weekend to Mateus, our beautiful manor house in the North of Portugal, and, knowing how polite Americans always are, I sent him a thank-you note, on a postcard of the house. So he invited me to lunch. It became regular: each day he would come pick me up at work (I was the senior assistant to the General Manager of Firestone Portuguesa) in Lisbon, take me to lunch, and drive me back to the office. Later in the afternoon, he would call and invite me for cocktails or dinner, pick me up, then take me home, to Cascais, where I lived with my mother after my parent's separation. We were courting. At some profound "heart level", I realized the seriousness of my involvement with David. He was indeed so different from anyone I had ever met. And I found myself in love, not "falling in love", but rather "rising in love".

On October 10, 1959, my younger brother Francisco was celebrating his 15th birthday. We invited David to come to dinner at home with my mother and brother. David agreed, but only on the condition that he would then be allowed to take me to the Casino to help him celebrate his October 11 birthday, his 31st. We had been seeing each other every day for two weeks, and David attempted not a hug, a kiss, even a touch. He was being a true gentleman. So, at about midnight that evening, I told him: "I am beginning to be very interested in you, and don't know how you feel about me at all."

David put out his hands, held both of mine in his over the table and said: "I love you very much, and would love to marry you."

"If," he continued, "we can overcome all the obstacles before us."

I asked: "What obstacles?" David said: "Well, we are of different nationalities, different religions, different backgrounds, and a different age". I smiled at him and said: "Those things don't matter! What I want to know is, will you kiss me when you take me home tonight?"

He did.

It turned out to be complicated for me to marry a foreigner, and a non-Catholic. Portuguese laws required many documents, all official, with official translations, and none would be valid three months after the date of issue! David went home to North Carolina and got his baptismal certificate, and all his other forms, in record time, and brought the required paperwork back to Portugal.

Then there was the issue of David himself. He was a heathen, a heretic. In other words, a Protestant. So when I requested we be married inside the Family Chapel, the Cardinal of Lisbon said: "Considering your family, we cannot make an exception, it would be a scandal. You must be married in the Sacristy." Not at the main altar.

And although my parents accepted David, my mother's parents were quietly concerned. Many years later my grandmother told me that it had been a "horrid shock" for her to adjust to the idea of having American great-grandchildren! Later she did get to appreciate and love David, as did my grandfather.

My mother asked David what he wished for, in return for all the hassles he had tackled in order for us to obtain the required paperwork for our marriage. His answer: he would like me to learn to play bridge. So, every evening, when I came home from work, the table would be ready, and the lesson would start!

There is a Palace in Lisbon, called Fronteira. It is one of the most beautiful palaces in all of Europe, and belongs to my first cousin, Fernando Mascarenhas the Marques of Fronteira. It was there, on April 23, 1960, in the tiny Sacristy next to the Chapel, on a beautiful brilliantly sunny day, that this Catholic teenager married an American businessman. Fronteira and Mateus are our family homes, very grand and beautiful; both are cultural foundations now.

Marriage, for me, meant a lifelong commitment. David and I both knew, at a very deep level, that we would be together forever. We knew our life would be a joint unfolding, a joint flowering, into ever more joyful loving. We had joined in heart and soul, and our past and future became intertwined.

Little did I know how nomadic our life would be from that day forward.

David brought me to the United States, to the small town of Oxford, North Carolina, where he grew up during the Depression. In the US I met my in-laws, became a United States Citizen, and had my eyes opened. As we traveled through very poor areas of the South, I saw waiting rooms titled: 'White waiting room' and 'Colored waiting room', and told David I thought it must be a rich country indeed, to have multiple waiting rooms even in such a small place, just to paint them in different colors. After recovering from his surprise, David explained to me that the signs were referring not to the color of the walls, but to the color of people's skin. It didn't make any sense at all to me! But so it was in the early 60's, in the United States of America. In Portugal we were class-conscious and color-blind.

So, where does a transatlantic Portuguese/American newlywed couple settle down? Everywhere! It was David's company, Mobil Oil, which kept us on the move: Tunisia, Nigeria, New York, Lisbon, Washington, Paris, Indonesia, Paris again... And because we moved so often, separating our lives from our marriage is impossible. Together, we faced challenges and enjoyed new places, faces and jobs.

So here is the story of our marriage, in the form of a travelogue.

Honeymoon in Rome

We went on our honeymoon to Italy. Rome was a delightful surprise! We had thought of going to Sicily but just couldn't leave Rome and all its wonders!

Tunisia

Our first posting was in North Africa. David became General Manager of Mobil's Tunisian exploration and producing affiliate there, which held exploration concessions jointly with a French national oil company. We loved Tunisia: the climate was perfect, the culture fascinating, the scenery fabulous, full of totally fascinating people, the food and wines were great. We made such good friends. But within a couple of months we had to face an unexpected challenge, a miscarriage, within a few months of our arrival. It was a boy, Philip Anthony Taylor. I went into a deep depression. My mother and little brother Francisco were visiting, but it felt to me like the end of the world. With David's love and tenderness, I pulled through.

And, before long, we had a beautiful daughter, Anne. Anne de Albuquerque Taylor. Motherhood filled me with bliss. I told David I wanted 12 children!!! She was born, not in Tunisia, where we were living, but in Portugal, where I went for the birth, because of the Bizerte crisis.

David improved his French a lot, because when he asked for a bilingual secretary, he got one; but instead of speaking English and French, she spoke French and Arabic. So we spoke French a lot, socially and at work.

Nigeria

But soon, when Anne was still a newborn, David was transferred 2500 miles further south, to Nigeria. Here, in the tropics, we spent almost five wonderful years, during which we had another wonderful little girl, Katie. Katherine Rowena Taylor. I worked for the Nigerian Government, ran a nursery school one summer and even learned to play Polo. Every day was full of discoveries, and I felt like a sponge with antennae. Moving from country to country was exciting, and challenging. It took a while to uproot, start from scratch in a new country, adjust to the climate (it's humid in Nigeria!) settle the family, make friends for the children, and help David succeed.

And David's career was sky-rocketing. At just 31, he was promoted to General Manager for marketing and exploration in Nigeria. He was responsible for over 1500 employees. Because of the importance of his job most of the people we saw socially (and it was an intense social life) were 25 or even 45 years older than I was. We made lots of friends.

Friends from those years are still in our life, like Professor Robert Collis and his wife Doctor Johanna Collis: they had liberated the concentration camp of Bergen-Belsen, and were extraordinary doctors, who opened hospitals and founded medical schools, in Ireland and Nigeria. He had discovered the cause of scarlet fever years earlier in Ireland. They both died in Ireland. Another friend was Sir Adetokunbo Ademola, then Chief Justice of Nigeria, who later introduced us to his young cousin who had married a young Ghanaian, who had just joined the United Nations. It was Kofi Annan, and he is still a good friend, with his beautiful wife Nane.

Oil was discovered in Mobil's offshore concessions during this time. World events ended our idyllic life in Nigeria. In 1966, in January, the

Prime Minister was murdered in a military coup. The entire post-colonial government was overthrown. A young nation – one of Africa's first post-colonial independent nations – was stumbling. Eventually these events led to a tragic 4-year civil war that killed over 3 million people. I cried for three weeks when we left Lagos, on April 2, 1966; and when we arrived in Lisbon my brother Fernando was at the airport and announced with joy the birth of his first baby, Teresa, who became my god-daughter. Those five years in Lagos, Nigeria had been a rich experience for us all.

We were fortunate and glad to be so adaptable.

United States of America

From Lagos we moved to New York. David went to several senior staff positions in Mobil's home office in New York City, which included two years as Assistant to the President and Secretary to the Executive Committee of Mobil's Board of Directors. In New York City we discovered the joy of great Opera, Ballet and Theatre. It is there that I started painting, going to a nearby studio for a few hours every morning.

The international life led us to decide to place our girls in the French International School System; that way we were sure they would have continuity, no matter where we went. And they learned their third language. Both of our daughters went from the New York Lycée Français to the Lycée Français Charles Lepierre, in Lisbon, the same Lycée that I had attended in the '50s. And they were in class with some of the children of my high school friends. We again appreciated what a fabulous educational system the French have, the reason why in every country there are so very many different nationalities attending. Children are guaranteed a place for continuing their education wherever they move to. It is fun that now, in 2014, our daughter Katie has had her son Felipe in the French school system here in Washington, DC, and he is doing very well.

Portugal

Starting in 1970, David was President and Managing Director of Mobil Oil Portuguesa, and its then overseas possessions, which were all under David's supervision.

Of all our foreign postings, Portugal turned out surprisingly to be the most challenging. We had come home to family, which can be the most difficult transition of all. My father decided to create a Cultural Foundation with our ancestral home of the Casa de Mateus. Many discussions took place between my father and my sister and her husband Jorge Goncalves Pereira and David and me about the by-laws, and about the aim of protecting Mateus for a long time to come, for itself and for future generations, protecting its history and beauty from political or personal danger and greed. My two brothers Fernando and Francisco were in Africa at that time for a few years. I became a permanent member of the Board of Directors, and still return at least once a year to Portugal, for the annual Meeting of the Fundacao da Casa de Mateus.

I was glad to be in Portugal for my father's last two and a half years of life and my maternal grandmother's last five. But work and family pressures seemed to accumulate, and depression became an unwelcome visitor for us both. After my father's death, family arguments about inheritance were dispiriting and heartbreaking for me. David was, as always, extremely supportive of me, as I was of him when he experienced the beginning of a breakdown, no doubt due to professional overwork. I enrolled at the School of Design and Fine Arts, and also at the Italian Institute, which were great fun.

As if that weren't enough, throw in another political upheaval: we were in Lisbon on April 25, 1974, when the Portuguese Revolution took place, ending over four decades of rule by Salazar and his successor, Marcelo Caetano. While it was quite chaotic, it was not bloody. It was the "Carnation Revolution," as people and soldiers traded flowers instead of bullets! After forty years of dictatorship, the "Portuguese Spring," as one would call it now, was quite exciting: I remember well the exuberance and excitement of that May 1st, the joy, the singing and shouting. So much hope filled the air, for better times, for openness and justice and freedom for all.

With the years many changes took place.

There were several different governments, including the communists; needless to say, this brought some anxiety for our family and friends, especially for my cousin, the Marquis of Fronteira, who had all of his lands occupied and it took over 15 years before they were given back, in dire condition.

By now my mother was calling David an itinerant political risk, since wherever we went there appeared to be a Revolution or a coup d'état, or some big turmoil! We'd had front-row seats for the Bizerte crisis in Tunisia in 1961, and the Biafra War in Nigeria started during our last year there, 1966. Richard Nixon was elected President in the US in 1969; we were on hand for the Revolution in Portugal in April of 1974. We came to live in the United States from 1975 to 1980 after the end of the Watergate scandal.

United States of America

We were relieved to be reassigned to Washington, DC. We easily agreed to buy a roomy house with a swimming pool, which could be a Portuguese Refugee Center if needed. And our girls continued with their education at the Lycée Français Rochambeau, in Bethesda, MD.

In 1975 Mobil had asked David to be the Administrative Manager of the Iranian Oil Consortium, of which Mobil was a member. Iran was still under the rule of the Shah; but following a visit to Iran, David refused the assignment, saying he was appalled by the atmosphere of corruption in the country at that time.

In later years he was quoted as saying "I can't say that I predicted the revolution, but I certainly wasn't surprised that it happened. My instincts told me not to take the job, and that proved to be the right move".

In Washington, DC, David was Mobil's Manager of International Government Relations, where he organized and coordinated these activities: advised the corporation on federal government initiative in the international area, and developed and implemented strategies to protect and promote Mobil's interests in these areas. He also represented Mobil with embassies, international organizations, academic institutions, trade associations and the like.

Once we were settled, we were looking for good American art for our large house. We were introduced to the now-famous artist Eugene J. Martin, and not only bought some of his art, but soon invited him to move in with us, so he would have the space to paint bigger pieces. We learned a lot with the very talented Eugene, whose devotion to art was impressive and whose vision was unique and full of humor. We began collecting many of his art works, and they surround us now.

It's perhaps at this stage, when the kids start becoming independent, when a couple starts getting anxious about the inevitable time when the house will be empty. Or maybe it is the need for the intense loving that motherhood brings in the first few years. When the girls were 13 ad 15 years old, a friend gave us a puppy. He was a tiny, adorable little black ball of fur that could fit in the palm of our hand; he was a silver miniature French poodle, and though he was small, his pedigree was almost as long as mine. Fusco.

But David didn't like dogs. He kept asking, "When is the dog leaving?" I looked into Fusco's eyes and couldn't imagine parting from him. I said, "How about, we send the dog away as soon as I am pregnant?"

Remember, I had said I wanted 12 children. So far we had only two. We were pretty far behind. I was giving David the option of a much more convenient choice: instead of 10 more children, we could just keep this puppy.

"That's blackmail!" he exclaimed. I could not disagree. "Yes, it is. But it's also a real choice." David filled the dog's papers with the American

Kennel Club. And he soon fell in love with little Fusco de Albuquerque Taylor. I can still see that puppy sitting very still and looking up at David, while David was having breakfast, and David smiling. Getting a dog was a transformational part of our relationship. Surely I needed the dog more than David did. I suspect that Fusco fulfilled a need in me: without that little poodle I may have clung a bit too closely to David.

By then our girls had grown: Anne, after The French Bac and a year at St Timothy's School, a fabulous all girls boarding school in Maryland, had gone to Georgetown University School of Foreign Service and then to England, and a couple of years later to Sarah Lawrence; and Katie went to St Timothy's, where she took the International Baccalaureate. She was then accepted in all ten top colleges to which she applied before picking Yale. A few years later, she would earn a double Masters, in Economics and Political Science, at Georgetown University.

In 1980, I took a fabulous trip to India, and then became an art dealer, importing art objects and paintings on paper, silk and cotton from India to the USA and Europe. With the help of an experienced friend in Washington, DC, my small art business grew and continues to this day.

Our girls were brilliant and successful, and David and I were ready to move to the next assignment: Paris.

France

Mitterrand had just won the Presidency - a great tragedy, from my mother's point of view. Living in Paris was even more fantastic than we had anticipated. David, still with Mobil Oil, was also involved with several West African countries, and we met again with old great friends and made new ones. David represented Mobil in a major joint venture project studying the feasibility of constructing an LNG plant in Cameroon. Mobil and the French company Total were the joint operating partners in the consortium which also included Shell, Elf, and the Cameroon National Oil Company. Due to changes in the international industry in the early '80s, and lack of further success in exploration, the project was terminated and David was transferred to Jakarta, Indonesia, as senior Vice President of Mobil Indonesia, responsible for all LNG Manufacturing and Marketing activities in what was then the most profitable affiliate in the worldwide Mobil network. This also involved travel and extensive negotiations with companies in Japan, Korea and Taiwan.

Both of our daughters came to visit us in Paris, and of course loved the beauty, the theatre, and taking courses at the Cordon Bleu School of Cuisine. Katie took time off from Yale for a one year course at the Ecole de Sciences Politiques.

Life was even better for little Fusco: one day while on a stroll on Avenue Montaigne, he met a young Mademoiselle of the same breed. We had a puppy two months later, whom we named Fofa.

Indonesia

Then, in mid-1983, we were assigned to Jakarta, Indonesia, and began the most fascinating experience yet: the people, the food, the culture, new friends – all exhilarating. The thousands of varieties of orchids led me to create an inner orchid garden, where I liked to sit, and read or meditate or watch the puppies play.

I took hours of Bahasa Indonesian every day. I had begun to collect Indian art, and now I became an avid collector of Indonesian art. I started importing Indonesian art to the US. We have since donated many pieces to the Textile Museum in Washington DC, but still have many on our walls.

Moving can be disorienting, for dogs as well as humans. Fusco and Fofa forgot they were father and daughter. She had a litter, on my lap, of whom we kept two. Sheba died a year later, but we kept the other, Shakti. We now had three adorable - silver poodles.

France

After just over one year in Indonesia (ending with an emergency appendectomy for me in Singapore), we were reassigned to Paris in 1984, and were able to negotiate returning to our previous apartment. We had the same address and phone number. David was to establish and manage an office responsible for Mobil's interests in a joint venture, exploration and production in Angola and Cameroon. Partners were French, Italian, and Yugoslavian oil companies and the National Oil Companies of Angola and Cameroon. But our return to Paris was made even more triumphant by the three silver poodles! We also took one of our maids with us, a wonderful woman called Ida Saleh, who was a great cook, a good worker and a good friend, and thanks to her I kept up my fluency in the Indonesian language.

In 1985 David asked to go with me to India, since I loved it so very much; we had a great trip, and after three fabulous weeks in India, going from fabulous place to fabulous place, we went to Egypt for the first time. So fascinatingly different!

United States of America

Retiring from Mobil in 1986, after 32 years of service, which had indeed kept us "mobile" for 26 years, we returned to Washington DC. to live. It was the year when we finally settled in one place. In 1987, David resumed an association he had begun in the late '70s with the Georgetown University School of Foreign Service as an advisor to the school's pioneer graduate program in International Business Diplomacy. Over the next ten years he served the school in a number of capacities, including Research Professor in International Affairs, Director of the Fellows in Foreign Service Program, and Senior Fellow in International Business Diplomacy. His graduate school course, Analysis and Forecasting, drew many exceptionally bright young people, some of whom are still our very good friends.

A few months after our return to the US our first grandchild, Gabriela, was born. Her mother, Katie, was at Yale, and I was there for the birth, and this special child has been a wonderful presence in our life for the past 27 years. And we discovered the immense joy of being grandparents! It is a special bond, an unimaginably intense bond, as we discovered with the arrival of each of our other four gorgeous granddaughters— Carolina, Joana, Leonor, and Sarah—who were born to our daughter Anne in Portugal, and our grandson, Felipe, born to our daughter Katie when she was living in Mexico. David feels, and I certainly agree, that grandchildren are God's way of giving parents a second chance: as parents we are so often busy and worried, but as grandparents we can enjoy every moment with each special grandchild.

A Spiritual Journey

And I began a different kind of journey, of the spiritual kind.

Before Gabriela's birth, David had brought to me the classic book The Varieties of Religious Experience, by William James. When I got to the chapter on Mysticism, I realized what I really wanted: the ecstasy of mystical union with the Divine.

How to achieve that? I went to the Light Institute in Galisteo, New Mexico, and had four days of Past Life Regression sessions, which transformed my way of being and seeing and thinking. I studied and trained and became a Past Life Regression Therapist and at the same time became a Rebirther. The practice of Rebirthing uses a technique of breathing which takes us to a non-ordinary state of consciousness, allowing us to see, and better understand, our life and its purpose, and approach Cosmic Consciousness, or the Union with the Divine within. I went to London to spend two months with my mother, who was dying of lung cancer, and found that my own meditative serenity was very helpful to her.

The following year, in February of 1990, I met Swami Chinmayananda. He was a rare, brilliant and articulate teacher of Vedanta, the most ancient and purest form of Indian Philosophy.

The 19th Century German philosopher Schopenhauer practiced it, writing: "In the whole world there is no religion or philosophy so sublime and elevating as Vedanta. This Vedanta has been the solace of my life, and it will be the solace of my death."

I like Schopenhauer: not only is his heart in the right place, and his thinking brilliant, but he loved and owned a succession of poodles throughout his life, and named them all "Atma", the Hindu work for the Higher Self, and Universal Soul, from which all the universe arises.

For three years, months at a time, I followed "Swamiji" around India and the world on his travels, as he planted and watered the seeds of wisdom in hearts and minds everywhere. Vedanta seeped into my whole being.

Swamiji had established many Vedantic institutions of learning, and under his umbrella was a wonderful project to empower rural peoples through the women, Chinmaya Organization for Rural Development, or CORD, which is a model of how to respect and inspire and help millions of people all over the world. Now, in India alone, 650 villages (with up to ten thousand inhabitants each) are a part of CORD. Dr. Kshama Metre is the creative, inspiring and inspired leader of it all. I decided that all the income from my little art business would benefit this organization.

This intensive spiritual life has changed David and me profoundly. He followed my journey with interest, attended retreats, and forged a loving, respectful and admiring relationship with Swamiji. David and I both cried when Swamiji died. The Vedanta philosophy brought us understanding and eliminated any possible religious differences. It has enabled our marriage, our relationship, to blossom within this ground of all Being.

That year, before meeting Swamiji, on September 29, 1990 our daughter Anne was married to Joaquim Manuel de Vasconcelos e Sa' Grave, at the Azinhal, in Evora, Portugal.

When Anne's first daughter, Carolina, was born, on May 22, 1991, I was in Delhi, unable to fly out because of the riots that followed the assassination of Rajiv Gandhi. Carolina, the prettiest doll with huge brown eyes and brown hair, and winning smile, came with Anne to see me and meet Swamiji in London two months later!

On June 12th of 1992, Anne gave birth to Joana, who is the first of her three beautiful blue-eyed girls. Her second blue-eyed beauty was Leonor, born on the 20th of November 1997.

On June 21, 1998, Katie married Antonio Gonzalez-Karg de Juanbelz y Orcacitas, at the Palace of Fronteira, in Lisbon, Portugal. They went to live in Mexico City. On April 27, 2000 they had a son, Felipe, our only grandson among many granddaughters, a perfectly marvelous boy!

In June of 2000, David had a heart attack, and a quadruple by-pass, followed by putting in a pacemaker. This happened instead of the 40th anniversary party we were giving at the Palace of Fronteira. Many of our friends came anyway, and celebrated without us!

The third blued eyed granddaughter, Sarah Anne, was born on February 28, 2002, slightly premature like all the others, but healthy and well.

We decided to give another anniversary party, for our 45th wedding anniversary. Many friends were able to attend from all over the world, and it was held at the Palace of Fronteira where we were married.

In 2007 we had a fabulous trip to Egypt, were accompanied by Anne and Leonor, Gabriela and our niece and goddaughter Sofia, who was an honorary member of the Taylor family. It was fabulous, even if in Luxor David had a detached retina. By the time we returned to Washington, DC, he had two surgeries but was unable to save the sight of his left eye. His right eye stayed pretty good, and he - enjoyed reading when he could.

In 2008, I took our granddaughter Carolina to India, wanting to share with her the beauty and richness of India, and also the work of our great friend Dr. Kshama Metre, and our Ashram there in Sidhabari in Himachal

Pradesh, while the rest of the world witnessed the fall of Lehman Brothers, and the beginning of the financial troubles still besetting the world.

We returned in time for the great celebrations of David's 80th birthday, attended by many friends and family members, at the Cosmos Club, in Washington, D.C.

In 2009 our daughter Anne's 20-year marriage to Joaquim ended, which saddened us all. And that year in November our niece and goddaughter Sofia died suddenly from a brain aneurysm.

We wept.

Fiftieth Wedding Anniversary

On the April 23, 2010, we celebrated our 50th wedding anniversary, at the Palace of Fronteira, and here is the poem David wrote for me:

A drop from heaven fell, near the Carolina shore
And ran its course into the East
To join the human ocean's roar.

And then a liquid pearl from Lusitanian rain
Melted in that sea and met the New World's main.

They joined themselves into a wave which leapt and
Danced across the world and glittered in the sun.
And late at night the moon looked down and smiled
At all they'd done.

But like all waves which run their course and
Melt back in the sea, as oceans end,
The moon goes dark, and time does cease to be.

And then, at last, the Eternal Mind
Will live in memory; the Eternal Heart
Will pulse for that which used to be.

And on God's face a smile will form
From thoughts of you and me.
I will love you forever!

     For Isabel from David, on our 50ᵗʰ wedding anniversary

In September 2010, David started having Hospice care here at home, a few months after having a stroke in Paris. He thought he wouldn't make it to his 82ⁿᵈ birthday, but he did. In mid-December the Hospice volunteers stopped visiting us. Now we spend even more time together, at home. We read. We prepared this book. We meditated together, we cuddled and we loved. We even traveled to Portugal together. We enjoyed each other. We are so very glad to have spent these past 54 years together! Now we understand the true meaning of love: deep commitment and devotion, impossible in a short relationship. We are aware of each moment of joy and loving, all through the day, even after death.

Life Now

On May 25, 2013 our first granddaughter Gabriela was married in Portugal, at the Palace of Fronteira, where we had been married. She married Joe Gurner, a very nice young man who is the Executive Chef at the Kennedy Center, so they live in Washington DC. It was a magically beautiful wedding and a lot of family was there, as well as friends from all over. Our granddaughters Carolina and Joana are living in Jackson Hole, Wyoming, working and studying. Our granddaughter Leonor is now at Saint Timothy's school, following the family tradition, and we enjoy her visits often. Our daughter Katie and Felipe live nearby in Bethesda, and Anne and Sarah who live in Portugal, visit when they can.

As we prepared for death, choosing the hymns, the texts to be read at our memorials, and so forth, we came to remembering that we all must die, and we never know when. That awareness was and is quite present and brings its own joy. And now, four years on, David celebrated his 85th birthday, with many family and friends.

The beauty of such a long life together is we find our hearts have kept opening, and the loving is greater, and the tenderness and appreciation are immense. Not only for each other, but for all of those who have been so important in our life, all of the family on both sides, and friends, colleagues, neighbors, everywhere.

Our granddaughter Gabriela, who had been living with us, said one time: "You two are the only couple I have ever met who truly love each other." We wish her an equally happy marriage to her wonderful Joe. We wish our two daughters and all our grandchildren a happy life and someone wonderful to share it with.

Each day we experience intense appreciation for each other, David and I, and for our life, so full of interest, and for our two daughters and six grandchildren, each of whom has enriched our life immeasurably. Each one has taught us how to love better and how to enjoy more, as have all the many members of our respective families and all of our many good friends all over the world.

To ALL, our deepest thanks.

PS: David died at home, in Isabel's arms, on April 25th, 2014, two days after celebrating their 54th wedding anniversary. He died without pain, to the sound of the Hallellujah Chorus, surrounded by love. He died as he had lived, with Grace and Dignity. He is deeply missed.

Reprinted with permission of the authors

THE SECRET TO DAVID AND ISABEL'S MARRIAGE?

THE POWER OF COMMITMENT

Commitment for David and Isabel was a big word: Commitment had to overcome social, political and religious barriers built over six centuries between the traditional aristocratic rules of Catholic Portugal and the modern American concepts of Protestant North Carolina. At a cocktail party in an elegant estate, in June of 1959,with the Royal Princesses of Italy in attendance, Maria Isabel de Sousa Botelho de Albuquerque, daughter of the Count of Mangualde, Vila Real and Mello met David Taylor. "He was so different from anyone I had ever met. And I found myself in love, not "falling in love" but rather "rising in love... And while he was searching for oil, I was surprised to find that we had both found \ something more valuable: each other." Our love and commitment transcended time and space, language and everything else, and we became closer and closer until we really had become one.

As they started courting, David said: "I love you very much, and would love to marry you...if we can overcome all the obstacles before us." I asked: "What obstacles?" David said: "Well, we are of different nationalities, different religions, and different backgrounds, and a different age." I smiled at him and said: "Those things don't matter! What I want to know is, will you kiss me when you take me home tonight?"

Isabel's grandmother told her what a "horrid shock" it had been for her to find out that her beloved granddaughter was going to marry an American. "And she just couldn't adjust to the idea of having American great-grandchildren! "

David and Isabel's marriage was going to be an amazing worldwide commitment, over more than half a century, that would know of no barriers. They would make friends and delve into the essence of every country they were assigned to work: Tunisia, with its perfect climate fabulous scenery

*fabulous, food and wines and interesting people; Nigeria where they wit-
nessed in 1966, the murder of the Prime Minister in a military coup, which
led to a tragic 4-year civil war, killing over 3 million people; Portugal with
its unexpected challenges in facing " the most difficult transition of all, after
my father's death, family arguments about inheritance were dispiriting and
heartbreaking" and the April 1974 Portugal's revolution, when 40 years of
dictatorship was thrown out the window. After Paris, they were assigned in
1983 to Jakarta, Indonesia, the most fascinating experience yet, where Isabel
started collecting orchids and Bahasa Indonesian art.*

*Then, onto a different kind of journey, of the spiritual kind. David
had brought to me the classic book The Varieties of Religious Experience,
by William James leading to a new goal,"the ecstasy of mystical union with
the Divine. All the time!" Isabel started to make pilgrimages to New Mexico
learning Past Life Regression and becoming a therapist. The following year,
she met Swami Chinmayananda, who became her Guru. For three years, she
followed "Swamiji" around India*

*"Every year we have returned to Portugal, to keep our commitment to
family. It took a long time for me to see myself and David as we are. And after
all those years, we find our hearts have kept opening, and the loving is greater,
and the tenderness and appreciation are immense". And now David is a total
constant presence in Isabel's heart and mind:*

*"In English, we say 'I miss you', but in French, we say 'You are missing
from me'(Tu me manques) and that is what it truly feels like, a big chunk of
you is gone, yet its memory lingers and enriches you forever..."*

CHAPTER X

Terry and Cal (51 years)

"The Fusion of Reality and Dreams"
By Terry Marder Kamin

About eight o'clock on work day mornings, Cal and I say, "good bye," for the day. The beds are made, the children off to school, we breakfast together. After coffee, I stand with my back against the kitchen counter. He comes close, touching. We embrace, standing silently for the moment. At this time, I might say to him, as I often do, tongue in cheek, "It's you and me against the world," or more often, I lean over and in his ear, say quietly, in almost a whisper, so that no one else in the world can hear the special invitation, "Let's run away." He, taking this in, after a few moments of consideration, responds, in all seriousness, "Where do you want to go?" I suggest a place of interest, like Hawaii or Tahiti. We banter back and forth about the positives and negatives of each place. He suggests a locale as well, maybe Japan. Our scenario complete, we are ready to face the day and enter fully the activities before us. It is in these few moments, playful in nature, taken in leisure, that our strong, intimate connection is reinforced. It says, "We stand together, as a unit. We're okay." Now enter the outside world with zest and joy and meet the challenge of the day.

Cal drives twenty minutes north to Sands Point to work on the construction of his latest building project. I drive twenty minutes south to Franklin Square, to begin the teaching day. It doesn't matter what I do after school, whether it is going to meetings, working late in the classroom, driving children to various activities, marketing, or swimming at the North Hempstead pool, when I make the right turn onto our street, Knolls Drive North, (where our driveway is in full view), if his car is in the driveway, I experience excitement. I anticipate being with him for the evening. I enter the house. He is sitting in the right hand corner of the couch reading his newspaper, the TV on, smoking (during those years before he kicked that habit). I sit down close to him. We hug a little, not necessarily talking or sharing. Then I proceed with chores and the preparations for dinner. About a half hour before dinner, I stretch out on the upstairs couch, read my newspaper and take a fifteen minute nap. We are separated in our physical space for a short time, as we enjoy essential down time and subsequent recharging, after the work day. However, the sense of completion and contentment in being together, with our family at home, is predominant.

It seemed important for us, always, to take the time, somewhat separating ourselves from whatever was going on around us, and in the course of each day, not just in the bedroom, to feel connection. This need for our marital unit to be close, but apart from others, was facilitated in other ways. Many of our vacations were private and planned purposely that way. Yes, we did take family vacations with our three daughters and, yes, we did go away occasionally with friends. Those times were grand, but the most memorable excursions were those where we went someplace interesting and spent time together and alone. That was incomparable. We were free of everyday responsibility. We could both dote on ourselves and each other while enjoying a rich exciting environment. We could be refreshed and nourished. We could fulfill ourselves with the space available yet be spontaneous. These were always the vacations that I didn't want to end. We had a memorable two weeks camping out and sleeping in our cranberry Pontiac Station wagon, with our regal Irish setter Reggie, through New Hampshire, Vermont and Maine. There was Mexico, a fascinating culture and an exotic, colorful environment which offered a romantic getaway. There was Israel, which was so emotional in its impact that it is still fresh in memory twenty five years later. There was a fulfilling visit to the Midwest. We went to Arizona, the Grand Canyon and then drove, as we always loved to do, to New Mexico. We were immersed in one of Cal's great passions; the history, art and culture of Native Americans. There was Paris, our last vacation alone. Cal was already showing symptoms of an illness that was later to take his life, but he was still viable and we were able to enjoy and appreciate all that an incomparable city offers. It was mesmerizing.

In addition to major trips, we made sure that, at least two or three times a year, we ran away for weekends. Sometimes we went upstate, to Mohonk Mountain House in New Paltz or to Woodstock. Sometimes, we chose Eastern Long Island, East Hampton or Greenport. The goal was always the same, to create a private space where we could be together and enrich our lives. During the years of hectic social life with friends, there were times when I would put a large "X" on a particular calendar date. Those were evenings devoted to "us" not social events. When it was inconvenient to be busy, I made up a fictitious couple with whom we had plans, and the reason why we were not available. Looking back on it now, it makes me laugh. Why didn't I just say to people, "Cal and I can't make plans with you because we just want to be alone, this weekend?" That's pretty simple, but maybe I thought it would not be received well. What it means to me now, as I look back on it, was how important it was to spend time nurturing our relationship as an entity that deserved our attention. It was a strategy that served us well.

Cal and I first met, as my best friend Roberta and I stood on the second floor landing of a flight of stairs, looking down. The downstairs bell rang. Our dates entered the foyer of the two family house, where the Moskowitz' rented an apartment. Roberta's family had spent a few weeks, during the summer, at the Pines in South Fallsburg, a Catskill Mountain vacation hotel where she met and dated a young fellow named Cal Kamin. He called her, in September, when they got back to Brooklyn and asked for a date. The arrangements were that he would bring someone for her friend Terry. We were excited to have dates for this first party with the new kids from Abraham Lincoln HS.

There were the guys at the bottom of the stairs, both handsome as could be, Cal and Norman. My eyes went from one to the other. There was no contest. I was immediately drawn to the fellow on the left. He was 5'10" with a sallow complexion. His hair was brown almost black, wavy and combed, as was the current style, into a dip on one side. His clothes hung gracefully hugging his body as if he had just posed for a magazine ad. His lips were soft, sensual and even from where I stood a distance away, he had magnificent dark brown "cow" eyes. When I said to Bobbi, "I like the one on the left," she responded, "That's my date." However, as the evening proceeded, it became clear that the chemistry was between Cal and me. When it was time to end the evening, it was Cal, not Norman, who walked me the block and a half to my apartment house, where I shook hands with him, thanked him and went inside. He did not ask for my phone number. This caused me anxiety for several days. When he ultimately called, we began to date. My seeing Cal did not create a rift in my friendship with Bobbi. She was a popular gal with no special attachment to Cal. What was unknown to me was shared in 2003, when Norman flew in from Arizona, for a visit, to see and spend time with Cal who had been diagnosed with dementia, in 1998, and was doing poorly. He related that, at the moment he and Cal, standing in the entry level foyer looked up, Cal leaned over and whispered to him, "Let's switch dates." Cal never told me and I smile that it took fifty years to emerge. What I did know was that our attraction was instant and mutual. It's still wonderful to have that anecdote as part of the history of that moment. I thank Norman for that. Was it love at first sight? No, not really. Love came later. It was an instant attraction, an immediate magnetic connection, exciting and undeniable. It was strong, chemical and psychological. It led, as it expanded, deepened and matured, into a love that ripened a process that developed over time.

The romance, because it occurred when we were so young, was rocky and sporadic. It was six years before we married. There were times we saw each other consistently for six months or a year, but other times when we broke up and were apart for, one time eight months and once for an entire year. Initially, we received negative feedback from both sets of parents and our families. This was because of our youth, not because they were against our choice. I can still hear my mother's voice, "You're too young. You're too young. First you graduate from college. Then you get married." I always responded, "Don't worry, even if I get married first, I will get my education." Periodically, Cal wanted to cut our relationship because he expected to be called into service. Those times were difficult for me. I cried a lot. Whoever I was dating, Cal was always in my thinking. He was always there.

The turning point came, senior year in HS. Lincoln was playing Stuyvesant for the city basketball championship. Cal and I had not seen each other for a year. I went to Madison Square Garden, with a date from Borough Park, Cal's neighborhood, primarily in the hope of seeing him. How in the world could any reasonable person ever expect to find someone in an arena as large as Madison Square Garden? Subsequently, Cal told me that he had gone to the game hoping against hope to see me and, yes, indeed, we did see each other. Our eyes met, even though we were a distance apart. My heart pounded. Lincoln won the championship by one point in overtime. The next week, I chose to send Cal a sympathy card which inspired him to call and the dating began anew.

The following year I attended Brooklyn College and began to date Jack, a Korean War veteran taking advantage of the GI Bill. Aware of a shift, Cal, felt threatened. He became serious, talking about our future together and we began discussing marriage. He had chosen not to go to Tulane where he had been accepted into the pre-med program, because he didn't want to be so far away from me, but was attending NYU. We were able to see each other several times weekly. It makes me laugh when I think about the lengths we went to in order to spend time together. During the week, Cal would go to classes in New York. Following that, he would work in his parents' paint and wallpaper store on Grand Street, in Williamsburg, late afternoon and until 9:00 at night. I was going to school evenings, transferring from day session, so I could work full time and save some money for a trousseau. He would finish work; drive his parents back to their home from Williamsburg to Borough Park so he could have the car. He then came to Brooklyn College to pick me up and drive me home to Ocean Parkway in Flatbush., a half hour away, so we could spend a few hours together. Our parents thought we were crazy to participate in such a rigorous routine but as all young lovers with the drive to spend time together at any cost, we knew better.

We became engaged one afternoon while Cal was at home with a virus. His parents were working in the store. I went to take care of him. While I was there, he told me he had a present for me. It was a small, rectangular tortoise shell evening handbag, a popular style of the time. It had my initials engraved elegantly in gold. It was most beautiful. He insisted that I open the purse. Inside was a black ring box housing the most exquisite diamond solitaire in a classic Tiffany setting. It was perfect in its simplicity as was everything Cal ever gave me. We married a year later.

As I remember it, there was no formal asking permission for my hand. There was just conversation after conversation about us, being together, being married. We did know that we wanted a large family, since both of us were only children. There is no memory I have of concerning myself with his character, or analyzing positive and negative traits, as one might do if older. I did not dwell on his drive to succeed, his ambitions, his perseverance or even what kind of husband or father he would be. I knew that he would be wonderful. I only wanted to be with him, was miserable without him and was happiest when we were together. Ultimately, he taught me the depth and breadth of what love offers, what you can give, receive and build in a relationship of respect. I had no concept, at that young age, what that would eventually mean, or what the scope of that would include, experienced over a whole lifetime, spanning the varying stages of marital life. It does not deny the recognition and acknowledgment that the other person has weaknesses and faults, as each individual does, but that the overriding understanding is one of acceptance. I am always in awe that as human beings we are capable of opening ourselves up and embracing those intense connections that offer such richness in life.

On January 30, 1981, our twenty-seventh anniversary, at my request, Cal wrote me a letter. I include a single paragraph as to me it signifies the sound and sense of his love, in his voice.

> *"My darling, my love for you is an ever present all*
> *encompassing experience of my every hour when away*
> *from you, even though thankfully this means only hours*
> *at a time, you are with me in my thoughts, for I can*
> *barely wait till we are together. Together means more*
> *just physical closeness for your presence is an*
> *enlightenment of whatever the prior minutes held for me."*

When we enter into marriage we bring with us a background of experience and expectations coming from our own family and our parents in particular. My parents were divorced when I was thirteen. It was the culmination of a five year struggle. Fortunately for me the first few years of my parents' marriage were normal, joyous years and I am grateful, that my early life was serene and stable. It gave me the base of emotional balance that served me well as an adult. In those years my parents were happy, although times were difficult financially during and after the depression. They were involved with family, all the aunts, uncles and cousins frequently getting together. We spent summers in Rockaway Beach sharing bungalows. My parents had many friends who came to bridge parties rather than spend money out or on baby sitters. My nickname, during those early years was "Mary Sunshine," which I think was indicative of my temperament and a basic lifelong focus on facing the direction of happiness. It serves one well in marriage.

The summer that my mother and I spent in Asheville, NC, when I was seven, was the critical turning point in their marriage. My father, a handsome, charming experimental person who considered himself a maverick, began a long term affair with a younger woman. She was single and a secretary in the office in the butter and egg market where my dad was an accountant and had been in love with my dad for a long time. Eventually, after the divorce, she became his wife and the love of his life. The years between the initiation of the affair and the divorce were difficult for me, as a young child and although I knew nothing about the situation it had its' effect on me and how I eventually viewed marriage.

The environment in our home was strained. My mother was aware of the affair since my father shared it with her. He did not want to break up his marriage. He loved and respected my mother, adored me and wanted her help. The years dragged on. The length of time coupled with my father's indecisiveness destroyed my mother. This plus the fact that no one in the family was aware of the situation created an environment and an experience of emotional isolation. At that time in cultural history divorce was a considered a 'shame'. Usually the blame was put on the woman. What did she do wrong, that her husband strayed.

During these years, there were no loud fights, only long periods of silence. My mother stopped talking to my father. These were deadly and contributed to the understanding I had, that in my marriage there would be no silences. Talk would be of great importance to me. Although there were a few times when Cal and I did stop talking, they were short lived. I would always initiate communication because silences were unbearable to me and at the same time unacceptable for children to witness.

One conclusion about marriage that came to me as a young adult was that I would never continue to live in such an unhappy situation, the way my mother had. Living in this kind of environment, I believed was not only seriously unhealthy for the adult, but also had detrimental effects on the rest of the family, which one had the responsibility to avoid. I used to say to Cal before we were married, "If I ever roll over in bed, look at you and feel I don't love you anymore, that's it, it's over." He shared with me that the flippancy of that statement was a concern for him before we got married. Fortunately, it never happened and looking back the statement seems ridiculously simplistic. However, the idea that marriage should be a mostly happy state of affairs persists and that if discontent is prevalent a couple needs to knock themselves out and work hard to do whatever needs to be done to accomplish the happiness goal if it is possible.

Ultimately, I believe that the most important aspect, I understood about marriage, taken from my mother's tragic experience, was that never, never can you take a happy marital state for granted. Joy does not float like a water lily in a pond of its own accord, without effort, just because a marriage exists. You bring everything you are into marriage. Marriage has cycles and rhythms, ups and downs that are natural, but that marriage needs time, work, nourishment and caring to thrive and survive the way you want it to. If you want to reap the rewards, you put in creative, thoughtful, loving efforts. Then the cup overflows.

Cal came to marriage being part of a family of strong stable marriages. His mother's parents were happy as were his parents. His mother and father were supportive of each other, were partners in business, spending all their time together, and strove to have a good life and provide a heritage for their only son. They believed you did what you had to do for your mate and for your family. Responsibility to family was high priority.

The main focus was not on, "me, me, me." I believe that I never, in all the years I knew them, heard that they had a fight or saw my in-laws angry with each other. The expectation that they passed to Cal was that being together is forever. I believe he benefited from the steady emotional rudder that steered his parent's marriage.

It's helpful but probably not essential to successful marriage that there be a measure of individual autonomy to balance common interests and the amount of time spent together. During our first few years, I was always registered in evening school classes working toward my degree, first, at Brooklyn College, and later, when we moved to Bayside and then to Manhasset Hills, at Queens College. Since we had Audrey, our first born eleven months after our wedding date, Cal stayed home those school evenings and took care of her and subsequently Cari, born two years and two months later and finally, Diane born four years after that. This gave Cal appreciable time with his children alone and me a major academic, intellectual interest outside the home, an excellent fulfillment in addition to raising children eventually leading to a career in teaching. Even today, I would recommend that mode of operation for young mothers.

While I was teaching, I generally maintained a separate school life including sociability. Cal was neither interested nor particularly involved. What I believe happens in that kind of situation is the time together is more exciting and the level of interest remains high.

When it came to common interests, we were in tune a great deal of the time. We were bridge partners. I bid well and he played out a hand expertly gaining that knowledge from the pinochle days with his father's family. We were tennis partners. Being tall and not afraid, I was good at the net. He was fast as lightning. The list of things we enjoyed together is long: fishing, gardening and hiking, being out in nature, cooking and camping, spending long days on various beaches. We both loved the theater, evenings at the opera, going to museums and for so many years, season tickets with good friends to the NY Philharmonic. We loved to travel to either big cities or be in natural environments. I suspect that it is an invaluable asset in any marriage to have a large retinue of common shared loves. It makes the time spent together easier. Instead of conflict about how to spend leisure time, there is cohesiveness.

But, as in any relationship, there were times when conflict emerges. He gets angry, we fight. He walks out of the house, slamming the door. Perhaps he is not coming back. There are the times when I thought, "Good, let him go." I must have been crazy to marry him and I certainly don't want to stay with him. It was at those times that a separation, a cooling off time is needed. We would go about our business apart, sometimes not speaking, sometimes speaking formally. We always slept together, no matter what was going on. The advice I received from one of my bosses, an attorney named J. Joseph Mehlberg, when I became engaged was, "Never go to bed angry and without talking it out." It is classic advice and still worthwhile. It was always in my thinking and I can say that it wasn't more than a few times, in our 50 years, that we were not able to manage non-stop communication until the problem was ironed out. We would get together after a little cooling off time. Usually, I was ready to initiate the first conversation. We had to agree to listen to each other and hear the speaker's point of view without screaming or interruptions. Listen, understand, compromise and then stay with it until it was okay and we were back on track. Rarely did it take more than one session of open, honest communication to come to terms with the issue at hand. Cal had an incredibly unique, sharp wit and a sense of humor that was an invaluable aid.

On some of the major issues that face couples, Cal and I were similar in our values and viewpoints. It made for less conflict. We did not fight about money at all. I don't believe in our entire life together Cal ever questioned me about anything I ever purchased. I also knew that, in the material world, all I would have to do was want something and ask for it and it would be mine. As a result, I was reasonably conservative with what I wanted, but it was a really delicious feeling to have. The issue that came up several times was what Cal would ask for or was willing to take from his parents, (who would give him anything). This was a little out of my value system. My parents didn't have much, so I became independent at an early age. I was not used to getting or receiving a great deal of material things from them, although my mother always did extend as much as she could. Ultimately, I let my discomfort go deciding that it was his relationship with his parents and not my business. My values should not intrude into this arena.

We never fought about family. Without any discussion that I can remember it was implicitly, "It's your family. What do you want to do? How do you want to handle this?" Then we supported each other. We had great responsibility to family, both our mothers being alone for many years, but because our sense of family values was the same, there was never an issue about it.

What might be a most significant area of marital functioning is that we did not have major conflict over sex. We seemed to have similar desires. Our rhythms and cycles were in sync and we saw sex as an expression of the love we had for each other, openness for experimentation, and a way to be intimate and as one. The fact that conception was easy was a plus which keeps sex life relaxed. Cal used an analogy to joke that I became pregnant so easily he had to wear gloves just to shake hands with me. Any problems that arose were in the normal range and were worked on with free and open communication and solved, in a reasonably calm manner, without anger or frustration.

The cause of our disagreements was in the way we wanted to raise our children. Cal was more traditional, more conservative and restrictive in his thinking. I was more laissez-faire. There was conflict during the young marriage because Cal had fits of temper that were volatile. If he became frustrated, he would become angry and lose his temper. Then he would lash out verbally. He would say outrageous things, he did not mean and regret it rapidly afterwards and apologize. For many years we had a dog, Reggie, an Irish setter, who was incorrigible. He was a magnificent animal. We all adored him, but he would behave badly. Cal would yell and threaten to get rid of him. The girls and I would be upset and eventually he would calm down. He would never have gotten rid of him. He loved him too much. Each incident was sheer torture for the family.

These outbursts of emotion were difficult to deal with. Once he physically smashed a hair dryer on the kitchen counter, (I don't remember the issue) so hard it dented the Formica. That dent remained as a sign of his temper. When he had these, my strategy was to walk out of the room, after I said what I needed to and leave him alone, until he calmed down and could converse reasonably. He was well aware of the problem and worked hard to gain control. As he matured, the problem subsided and by the time he was in his forties it was minimal.

Depression caused some of the darkest times, in our marriage. They were the result of Cal's expectations of himself in terms of what he wanted to accomplish financially, coupled with business downturns. As a builder, he was always undercapitalized. When there was the end of a project with nothing new beginning on the horizon, there were lean times. That particular cycle happened several times. Cal would become depressed, which took its toll on the whole family. He would be uncommunicative and withdrawn. We drew apart emotionally. They were painful times. He fought to get out of the abyss. I worked hard to be supportive and we both did work to think of ways out, of ideas, of solutions. Eventually, he always did find another project to develop, would get excited with the planning and things would turn around.

One of the worst of these times was when, during a long dry period, he decided to go into a business he knew nothing about. It was the garment industry and it was a decision made in weakness, at a time of desperation. After a horrendous year, Cal being depressed most of the time and hating each day's work, nearly having a nervous breakdown, he knew he had to leave that business. He walked out with my total support.

An incident which caused an explosion, one time, brings back painful memories primarily because I was at fault. It was the day following a social Saturday evening. It had been an elegant dinner party in Sands Point. Liquor flowed all evening. Dinner was late. I had too many cocktails, with not enough food. I was spending time talking to one of the guests, not giving my husband attention. Cal felt that I was being flirtatious, became infuriated and insisted that we leave the party and return home. It was one of the only times that he, the next day, walked out of the house, staying away for several hours without saying where he was going, or if, or when he was coming back. I was beside myself. I knew I was at fault but it was past history. I couldn't turn the clock back. I didn't know what to do. I apologized. He was hurt. I cried. He became frustrated. I entreated. He didn't care. I promised. He was unresponsive. Eventually, when he returned from his escape, and the time passed that day, he calmed down, accepted my apology with my regrets. He let it go. We went on. I was the wiser for the incident and understood that in my marriage, one of the things that was ultimately important was to own the behavior that belongs to you, even the painful stuff. If you, in fact, were wrong, say so, admit and apologize. You cannot change reality. What you can do is be honest, clear the air, say it like it is and in this way create a better future by doing the right thing and then learning from a mistake.

There were many difficult times during the years with family illnesses. We survived the death of his parents, my parents, and the tragic death of my cousin Toby at the age of 45. There were many incidents and problems with three daughters growing up. We were inundated with teenage issues during the hippie era. However emotional, they did not cause dissention in our marriage. For the most part, we stood together, and worked as partners forming a team to deal with these crises. Whoever was the strongest emotionally on a particular issue, lead the way. The other party acknowledged and accepted the guidance. It did not cause conflict.

On one level, part of the solution is just going day by day, sometimes through instinct. Hopefully, that instinct is positively based. The other part and maybe this is the crux of the situation is the support one partner gives to the other and the support one feels from the other. Whatever comes up, you approach it as a team. Whatever your individual agendas are, they are secondary to the need of the two together. There is invaluable strength feeling support from your mate. That support came from the base, forever present, of love and respect. Cal knew, always, that I would support him in whatever he wanted to do. On the other hand, I knew, in my heart he would never want to do anything out of our mutual value system therefore giving me the confidence to feel that way. I also understood that Cal would back me in any person decision. In fifty years he never said, "No," to me.

At one point after many years of teaching and thirty credits beyond the Master's degree, I considered going for a PhD. Columbia University offered a doctorate in Gifted Ed, the field I was in. I had always wanted a doctorate. I weighed all the pros and cons. Years and years of course after course, time away from family, leaving Cal a few evenings a week. The expense would be appreciable. The time needed to complete studies intense. The decision was mine and during every step of that decision making process, I knew that Cal wanted me to do, whatever was best for me. That would be fine with him. He never said one word to dissuade me from that course, if that was what I chose. Ultimately, I decided against the program, but always appreciated the sense of personal freedom I had with my husband and within my marriage.

If I look back dispassionately, from third person perspective, what I say is, "Two kids got married. They didn't acknowledge that they were kids. They blundered into marriage overflowing with passion and a positive desire to build a future together. In the blink of an eye they had three beautiful, magnificent daughters to raise and a full blown complex, volatile family life for which they were never expertly prepared. Yet, with instincts at work, intelligence intact, maturity emerging as experience was gained and love as the highest value, they created a life full, rich and well worth both the living and remembering."

In order to term a marriage successful, I believe, each individual must feel and know that the relationship has been for the most part overwhelmingly joyous and reasonably easy. The dark, difficult times were weathered supportively with the marriage emerging intact, sometimes stronger. There is a feeling of the fullness and completion of the experience along with an understanding and recognition that being together was the best and richest way to live.

When people are together with the right person, it is very clear to them that this is so. It is sometimes referred to as being, "Soul mates." How you find that, I don't know. Personally, I believe it is meant to be. Others believe it is luck. You could make the case either way. Science has little to do with it. When you are with the right person, you know it in your heart, just as you know when you are not. A while ago, I asked a friend who was married for twenty three years before her divorce, when she knew the marriage was a mistake. Her reply, "As I walked down the aisle, I knew." It was not the only time I have heard such a response. For me the understanding was always that there was no one else I would rather have shared my life with but Cal, that I was always in the perfect place being married to him and that it was right, always right. If I think about whether I would or would not do it over again …without a second's hesitation the answer is a resounding, "Yes, absolutely, in a heartbeat."

THE SECRET TO TERRY AND CAL'S MARRIAGE?

THE POWER OF LUST

For Terry and Cal, it was immediate, unbashful, physical and passionate attraction the minute they met! "I was immediately drawn to the fellow on the left... His hair was brown almost black, wavy and combed, as was the current style, into a dip on one side. His clothes hung gracefully hugging his body as if he had just posed for a magazine ad. His lips were soft, sensual and even from where I stood a distance away, he had magnificent dark brown "cow" eyes... What I did know was that our attraction was instant and mutual. It was an instant attraction, an immediate magnetic connection, exciting and undeniable. It was strong, chemical and psychological. "

Life was not going to be easy for Terry and Cal. Cal was often angry and argumentative, and would leave Terry at times, slamming the door behind him. There were also to be family illnesses and tragedy...and three daughters to raise. No matter what would go on in their lives from thereon, Terry knew that: "I only wanted to be with him, was miserable without him and was happiest when we were together."

Both Terry and Cal were very open about the importance that sex played in the success of their marriage: "What might be a most significant area of marital functioning is that we did not have major conflict over sex. We seemed to have similar desires. Our rhythms and cycles were in sync and we saw sex as an expression of the love we had for each other, openness for experimentation, and a way to be intimate and as one. The fact that conception was easy was a plus which keeps sex life relaxed. Cal used an analogy to joke that I became pregnant so easily he had to wear gloves just to shake hands with me."

Sexual desire has been recognized as a primary force in the union of man and woman since biblical times. Genesis 2:24 says: "That is why a man leaves his father and mother and is united to his wife, and they become one flesh." Millions of books, novels, films have been published and produced over the centuries on the power of sex. In her book, 'Why We Love: The Nature and Chemistry of Romantic Love', biological anthropologist Helen Fisher proposed three core brain systems for mating and reproduction, namely lust (sex drive or libido), attraction (early stage intense romantic love) and attachment (deep feelings for a long term partner). In 2004, while at Rutgers University, she studied men and women who had just fallen madly in love using fMRI brain scans. Men generally showed greater activity in visual areas of the brain whereas women showed more activity in areas linked with memory recall. As a rule, the brain chemistry appears to shift as our relationship grows over time. Terry and Cal seem to have managed to maintain throughout their marriage a very intense sex drive which kept their union fresh and exciting despite the obstacles.

Sex in marriage can be a double-edged sword. "Sex can be a wonderful cementer or a terrible wedge" for relationships, according to Dr. Linda Banner, Ph.D., a licensed sex therapist who practices marriage and relationship counseling at Stanford University Medical School. In my practice, I often see older couples eager to maintain a healthy sexual life and requesting advice and therapy to fulfill their sexual needs. The key to sexual fulfillment is to recognize and accept realistic expectations and to find a partner eager to participate, to give and to take.

Terry and Cal were always able to communicate their needs to each other, no matter what else was happening in their lives. And, they were always eager to participate! "For me the understanding was always that there was no one else I would rather have shared my life with but Cal, that I was always in the perfect place being married to him and that it was right, always right."

Cal and Terry were to be blessed with fifty one years of blissful sex, many arguments, lots of fights and ultimately wonderful moments of true happiness.

CHAPTER XI

Robert and Cinde (51 years) ...and Lilliana! (13 years)

"For Twice in My Life"
Serendipity

I couldn't take my eyes off of her as she crossed the street.
I was entranced by her strong assertive New York woman stride.
And, she had a captivating exotic beauty.

It was a warm summer day in 1950 and I had a couple of weeks before I boarded a freighter to take me to India for post graduate work at the University of Bombay. To pass the time I decided to relax at a Catskill resort for the weekend. I was waiting with a vacationing group on the corner of 6th and 16th in Manhattan for the limos to take us to the resort. And then she came across the avenue. I was delighted to discover that she also was going to the resort. On the trip up we talked and talked. And continued far into the night and for the following two days. Our attraction took on lightning speed. We had a communion of body and mind. We lived a magical fairyland of discovery. We enthralled each other and felt as if we were looking down on the sky.

By the end of the weekend I knew I was in trouble.

And then back to Manhattan where we spent the week exploring New York City and each other. Central Park, a smoky jazz nightclub on 52nd street, Greenwich Village, a walk in the rain on the lower east side, San Carlos Hotel, Camp Unity. All the planets were aligned and we had feelings of exuberant ecstasy. By the end of that week we were both open-eyed at what we had created. Like new wine in fermentation, we bubbled with excitement. The outside world became a haze. I saw and thought only of her. When I first met her it was "I". Then suddenly it was "We".

One week after we met, I proposed. And she accepted. At that moment I had an epiphany and total unbridled euphoria. Unqualified commitment. I was never so sure of anything in my life.

A week later, I left for India.

Our courtship consisted of many, many letters back and forth. Her name then was Henrietta — which we later changed to Cinde — short for Cinderella.

I was 22, she 26.

More about that later.

But first let me go back and tell you where both she and I came from.

Bob before Cinde

I was born in Kansas in 1928 of German and Danish stock.

My ancestors came to Kansas in covered wagons. On the farm of my uncle, I learned how to ride horses and bring the cattle in from the fields. I milked cows and drove the farm tractor. I helped to butcher hogs and calves. The farm had no electricity. We used coal oil and Coleman lanterns for light at night. I learned how to shoot with the family 22 rifle. My aunt and I made soap from grease and lye. I helped feed and attend to the cattle, horses, swine, and sheep. I assisted with the delivery of their "babies"; a most informative and valuable experience. We cured hams, sausages, and beef in the smoke house.

I was the youngest in the family with three sisters. I had exposure to many "feminine" things. I was accepted as an equal and I reciprocated. I had no concept of females as the "weaker sex". I combed my sisters' hair, helped with their makeup, and rubbed their backs during their periods. They and my Dad patiently taught me how to be a strong male without domineering the opposite sex. Presents to the children were not sex oriented. I recall one Christmas, for example, when, among other presents (like a bicycle), I got a doll and a recipe book, and one of my sisters got a bat and ball.

My Dad was the strongest influence on my life at the time. He was the Vice President of a mid-west oil company who had been a hands-on farm boy who relished both physical and mental labor. He introduced me to mechanics and carpentry when I was about two years old. He seldom admonished me for childish thoughts or behavior. As he put it "life itself will straighten things out". Years later he delighted in instructing me in the ways of business and finance. He and his father were involved with the Indian tribes in Kansas. My grandfather had deeded a portion of his land to the Kickapoo Indian tribe.

And then, with the ongoing depression of the 30's and the disheartening dust bowl of Kansas, Dad decided it looked much better for us over the horizon. We left for the lush greenness of Oregon.

Oregon

When we moved to Oregon in 1939 our entire family worked in the fields picking fruits, vegetables, and hops. The money was all contributed for our family expenses. Although we were far from poor, Dad wanted to make sure we had enough money to start a new business. After months of searching and negotiating, Dad put everything we had in "hock" to put a down payment on the Ford dealership in the town of Albany. Pure guts and risky but he built it into a very successful business.

Albany was a simple, comfortable, provincial town. Population of 5,280 (the number of feet in a mile). One black family and one Jewish family. I didn't view them any differently than anyone else. Until high school I thought a Jew was just a different kind of Christian (like a Lutheran or a Methodist). Such was the naiveté of one from the free and open life in the "wild west", untouched by the biases of large cities. One of my childhood buddies was the only black boy in town. I was a boy scout and went hiking and camping in the wilds of Oregon.

War time: 1941-1945. The US Army built Camp Adair some 10 miles from Albany. With 20,000 soldiers, the camp brought new excitement and some sophistication to the town. Rationing during the war. Red stamps for meat and butter. Blue stamps for canned goods and clothing. And only a few gallons of gas a month. Recycling of everything — paper, tin cans, grease, wood, glass. Dad and I were "air raid wardens" watching for enemy aircraft. Our "post" was a 100 foot tower on a high hill. We watched and listened for aircraft. We could identify, by sound, as least 20 types of aircraft. At night almost all lights were blacked out throughout the area as we prepared for a possible Japanese invasion. We studied road maps for our possible retreat path to the mountains east of us. We were only some 50 miles from the coast!

At 15, after a year of self-study, I took a government test and received a Federal Communications Commission First Class Radio license. I've been told I was the youngest in the U.S. to get the license. Shortly after that, I was hired as an announcer/disk jockey for radio station KWIL. A year later I was promoted to Chief Engineer. Everyone else with a license had been drafted! For several years I worked the 6PM to 12 midnight shift at the station. I worked "combo" (i.e., both announcer and engineer). Most of the time I was the only person at the station in the evening. News, sports, drama, disc jockey (DJ) - all live announcing. Audiotape not invented yet. I selected the records and determined the program formats. I learned how to plan ahead and work under the psychological pressure of sole responsibility. I set up and announced the first live band radio remotes from the local nightclub/dancehall (one night stands by Jack Teagarden, Woody Herman, among others).

I was intrigued with writing about technical subjects. My first nationally published article appeared in the magazine Radio Craft. I was 15 years old. It was about the design of audio amplifiers. On high school graduation, I received the national Bausch/Lomb science award.

Then to Oregon State University, 1946-1950. Degree in Science with a major in Physics, minor in Philosophy.

I was class president of some 5000 students and a member of Sigma Phi Epsilon fraternity. The chapter had the top academic scholarship on the campus for 21 consecutive years. I objected to the fraternity's White Christian policy and made a formal application to pledge a Jewish friend and Bill Maxwell, a black. Both were rejected. In symbolic protest I moved out of the fraternity house. Bill later got his doctorate from Harvard and is now internationally known and respected.

In college I was involved in theater, music, and radio plays. I did a weekly radio interview program and wrote several science fiction dramas that were broadcast on the national educational radio network. I took flying lessons and got a pilot's license.

Political awakening. I was president of the Students for Democratic Action (a student branch of the Democratic Party). It was the beginning of the McCarthy period. I had political conflicts with the college president. He objected to my support of alumnus, Linus Pauling (who later was the only person in history to be awarded two Nobel Prizes). The head of the Oregon Democratic Party wanted me to run for State Senator. In his words I was "young, new blood, at ease on a stage, politically savvy" etc. I declined. I wanted to travel and to write.

I drove to New York in the summer of 1949. Among other activities, I was the MC at "17 Barrow" a Greenwich Village night club. Song and stand-up comedy. I also went to the School of Radio Technique to study announcing. Milton Cross, the "voice" of the Metropolitan Opera was my teacher. Dialects, commercials, drama, news, interviews, etc. At night, I picked up some income as a drink "mixer" in back of the bar at the Latin Quarter Night Club on 47th Street in Manhattan. (Lou Walters, father of Barbara Walters owned the club).

Back in Oregon, I built racing cars and raced on both tracks and drag strips. I held the US speed record for "hot rod" drag racing (for about a month) in the late 1940s. 124 miles/hour.

At Oregon State I was in the naval officer training program for two years, then I transferred to the Marine Corps program for two more. On graduation in 1950 I was commissioned a Lieutenant in the USMC reserve.

I had a number of foreign student friends at the University and was particularly interested in India as the first major country emerging from foreign domination. Since I was not being called up for service in the Marine Corps I decided to pursue post graduate work at the University of Bombay.

I travelled to New York to wait for a freighter to ship out to India. To pass the time I decided to take a short weekend "vacation" at a Catskill resort.

It was August 25, 1950 and lightning struck!

Now, let me tell you about Henrietta (who later became Cinde).

Henrietta before Bob

Henrietta's parents were born in Latvia, then part of Czarist Russia. When the pogroms came, the Cossacks went through the villages burning the houses of the Jews. One of these times her mother burrowed into a snow bank with her parents, hiding until the Cossacks rode away. Her father, who was forced into the Czar's army, deserted as soon as it was apparent that one of the main tasks of the army was to harass the Jews.

In general, their life in Latvia had very much the flavor of Fiddler on the Roof. Her Father was the philosophic, ever-bending, "If I were a rich man", wanting to give his children everything he could. Her Mother was the matchmaker, the entrepreneur, trying to turn a penny to make life a little more secure. Shortly after, they made their way through a tortuous escape path and arrived at Ellis Island in 1906.

Henrietta Schlossberg was born in the outback swamps of Alabama in 1924. She was youngest in the family with four brothers. The day the family moved into a little shack overlooking a river, there was a sign on the outhouse door, "Get out of town Jews. KKK". Her brothers reported seeing, on several occasions, lynched blacks hanging from trees.

It became obvious that a better life lay elsewhere. A year and a half later the family moved to Louisville, Kentucky where Henrietta spent much of her teen age life.

In the early years in Louisville the family lived in a series of houses. Most of the moves were caused by the necessity to skip out on the rent. Her mother tried a number of small businesses, selling clothing and pots and pans. Her father became an independent milkman with his own truck. Finally, with some modicum of financial security, they rented out rooms. Henrietta said that they always had a variety of weird strangers in their house.

At one very difficult time for her parents — when she was about 3 years old – Henrietta was put into a charity children's home. A dismal place. A humiliating experience. She wet the bed because she had been given boys' underwear, which she couldn't figure out. They put her in diapers and paraded her in front of all the rest of the children!

When Henrietta started public school, she began to blossom. By the 4th grade, she was a straight A scholar. Her youngest brother coached her in acting and speaking (to get rid of the southern accent). When Henrietta was 10, she had the lead role in a radio play on the local NBC station.

As for being "Jewish", her parents, while not exactly freethinkers, were also not orthodox. They followed some of the rituals but were far from dogmatic. Her father would often secretly buy non-kosher meat (it was cheaper) about which her mother pretended not to know. Her mother — rather than having three different sets of dishes (for milk, meat, and holidays) — would simply use non-absorbing glass dishes (which they got as prizes at the movie theater).

Junior high school was a time of awakening. Henrietta was an avid reader - many hours at the library. Latin and English were the favorites. Her interest in acting was growing and she took every opportunity to get on stage. Her mother bought an old piano and Henrietta taught herself to play it and to read music.

She sailed through Louisville Girls High School. (High schools were segregated by sex at the time.) Acting, orchestra (harp), literature, journalism, Latin, English. She graduated in 1941.

Near the end of her senior year in high school, the orchestra director of Transylvania University in Lexington talked to her. He had heard that she played the harp and they needed a harpist for the orchestra. She was offered a scholarship and with the income from a job in the school cafeteria she paid for her tuition. Transylvania was the first university founded west of the Alleghenies. George Washington and John Adams were major contributors to the founding fund. The main curriculums of the university were the arts, medicine, and law. They also had a large theology department for the Christian ministry.

Her major was English. Her main activities were theater, journalism, and music. She was the only Jewish girl on campus. They didn't quite know what to do with her. In spite of some of the obvious, but unstated, anti-Semitism, Henrietta was elected president of the student body. She graduated with honors and was included in "Who's Who in American Colleges and Universities".

New York

Within two weeks after college graduation, Henrietta arrived in New York intent on an acting career. However, agents weren't exactly flocking to her assistance. To make ends meet, she took a job as the midnight clerk at the Park Central Hotel. After six months, her mother died and she went back to Louisville to stay with her father. She was in Louisville a year and a half.

During that time, along with some of her friends, she taught ballroom-dancing at Arthur Murray Studios. They had good report with their students but management was not happy. Henrietta and the others were chastised for teaching too quickly and not stringing along the pupils. After their wages were withheld they won a law suit against Murray and won back pay.

Then back to New York. After more than a year of pounding the bricks for acting jobs and dozens of auditions, it didn't work out. Finally she got a real job. She was hired by Pageant Magazine as the "slush" editor. Her job was to read unsolicited manuscripts and to separate the wannabe writers into "yes", "maybe", and "no". In a year there were only four "yeses" that got into the magazine.

Henrietta's next job was as the Research Editor for the Encyclopedia Americana. The work was prestigious, exciting, and challenging. And she loved it.

But then something momentous and serendipitous happened.

Her brother was business manager of a national weekly newspaper. He suggested, one summer day, that she might enjoy going for a weekend outing in the Catskills with the editor and staff. After some initial hesitation, Henrietta agreed and headed to 6th and 16th for the limousine. She was 26.

While standing on the corner she met a young man. His name was Bob. It was August 25, 1950.

India

After two weeks exploring with Henrietta, getting engaged, and planning for the future, I left for India on a freighter to Morocco, Tunisia, Spain, Egypt, Jeddah, Djibouti, Pakistan, Ceylon, and finally, Bombay.

When I arrived in India, and was matriculating at the University of Bombay, I was shocked to learn that they would require me to take two years of under graduate work before beginning post graduate studies! It turned out that the University, which operated under the British "Cambridge" rules, considered an American university degree as being two years "behind". I declined admission.

Not to waste the trip, I traveled throughout India (Delhi, Kashmir, Madras, Calcutta,). I contracted malaria in a remote village in central India and was unconscious for several days in a mud hut "hospital". Swimming in the Ganges probably didn't help! Later, at the request of the young people of the village, I drew up plans for a simple hygienic hospital building, as well as a design for a bridge over the river (rather than having to use a poled raft). Although the five village leaders (the Panchayat) rejected the ideas, the young people asked me to draw up the plans and promised that someday they would build them.

Back in Bombay, I became a stringer correspondent for a couple of American newspapers. Among a number of articles I wrote was a half-hour private interview with Prime Minister Jawharlal Nehru. This was during the Korean War and peace discussions were at a stalemate. To my surprise Nehru offered the "good offices of the Indian government" to negotiate a peace settlement. I sent my "scoop" to a number of press organizations around the world. Not one picked it up. Apparently they were not about to believe or trust a no-name reporter with such an ice-breaking story.

I had a job offer from Radio Ceylon as an announcer and disk jockey. Radio Ceylon was the most powerful broadcast station in the world. The signal could be heard from Japan all the way around to Brazil. They were very excited to have a real American disk jockey on the station. I rented an apartment for Cinde and me in Columbo, Ceylon. I wired her to get ready to come over. Then — the job fell through! The Ceylon parliament had just passed a law that no foreigners were allowed to work on government projects.

For several weeks I was the MC at the nightclub of the famous Taj Mahal Hotel in Bombay with a dance group called the "London Starlets." The "Starlets" returned to London and I was out of a job.

On a daily basis I would buy candy and cigarettes from American seamen aboard docked USA ships and sell them on the black market for next day's rent and food. I had run out of money and was "on the beach".

I was disgusted with the entire scene. Dead-ends everywhere. I decided that India and I were not right for each other. I applied to the American Consulate in Bombay for work-a-way passage on a freighter back to the States. Finally a ship came in that needed a seaman. I boarded and shipped as the "mess boy" on the US Steel Advocate. The crew and I had a lot of fun. For example, they enjoyed saying, "Lieutenant Sir, I want my steak well done and more coffee right now!" We sailed to Calcutta and several other India ports and then back up the Suez Canal, through the Mediterranean and finally to Baltimore.

1951 to 2002

Cinde met me at the ship in Baltimore. February 3, 1951. Snow on the ground. Cinde was the only person on the dock looking way up at this great big ship. I got fast customs clearance because she was there. Then up to New York. A week of preparations for the wedding. Mother and Dad arrived from Oregon. Wedding at Cinde's apartment. February 12, 1951.

We drove cross country to Oregon. She had never been west of the Mississippi and was astonished at the enormous open expanse of the country. On the trip we changed her name from Henrietta to Cinde. She never liked the name Henrietta which her friends reduced to "Hank"! We agreed that Cinderella was perfect since that was how I felt about her. But it sounded too pretentious. So, I wrote "Cinderella" on a strip of paper and took out scissors and cut between the "e" and the "r". That's how her new name became "Cinde".

In Oregon I drove a gravel truck while waiting for Marine Corps orders. Cinde worked as a "car hop" at a drive in. I received no Marine Corps orders to report, so we bought a house trailer for flexibility in assignment and left to seek our fortunes in San Francisco.

A long job search in San Francisco finally resulted in a job at NBC Television as an engineer.

During the next several years I was the technical director for a number of television "firsts". Almost all television was "live" – videotape had not yet been invented. Industry was in its infancy. We innovated, invented production methods, and experimented with new program ideas. Very exciting! On the "Wide Wide World" program with Dave Garroway sitting in a New York studio, I was the technical director in San Francisco for the first live TV program from an in-flight airplane and later from a submerged submarine. Then, the first use of live coast-to-coast television via micro-wave for the Japanese Peace Conference in September 1951. Many other ground-breaking television programs like The Home Show with Arlene Francis, Hugh Downs, and Barbara Walters. The first live side-by-side pictures of the Golden Gate Bridge in San Francisco and New York Times Square. Etc. Etc. These were all in black and white, until I helped to set up the first color camera on the west coast. It was a heady time.

Cinde and I worked for a couple of years writing a 170 page book, "Out of the Horse's Mouth". We used newspaper clippings (from papers of the full political spectrum) to illustrate how the US and other countries were surging toward a terrifying nuclear disaster. Given the political clime during the McCarthy period it was obvious why we could find no US publisher willing to step out of line.

During this time Cinde and I started a record company "Americord", primarily to produce American folk and ethnic music. We released a number of records including those with Stan Wilson and Pete Seeger. Cinde and I wrote and produced a number of pilot television programs for NBC including "Chalktalks", an elementary science show for adults. We taught courses at the California Labor School, a union supported school in San Francisco. I taught science courses and Cinde taught drama and acting.

We were involved in the peace movement in the early 1950's. Basically "anti-McCarthy" and "ban the atom bomb" activities.

In 1952, without previous notice or warning, I was given an "other than honorable discharge" from the Marine Corps. I requested and got a "hearing". It was an Alice in Wonderland kangaroo court. The charges were read to me but I was not permitted to challenge them, nor would they disclose the source of the accusations. Apparently they related to my political activities in college. They were about 10% true and 90% fabrication. For the next 12 years I went thru the legal machinery and finally had a legitimate hearing in Washington DC before the Naval "Supreme Court". I got a complete reversal, an expunging of the derogatory files, and an honorable discharge signed by the Secretary of the Navy.

In 1956, I left NBC to start - with three others - the educational television station KQED (PBS) in San Francisco. I became Director of Engineering and Operations. KQED was the fourth PBS station on the air in the country. The station had no studio and I and my engineering group along with volunteers (none had any previous television experience) built the studio with donated surplus equipment. In two years we became the major production center for PBS and produced hundreds of educational programs. During this period I also designed the educational TV network for the state of Hawaii.

Cinde felt that she also should know the technical end of radio and television. She subsequently studied and passed the federal exam for a First Class FCC License – one of the few women to do so.

We were both involved in on-camera activities as well as those behind the lens. She had a very successful weekly children's television program called "Pixie" that ran for 26 weeks. She was the Pixie - a playful forest elf who told stories in front of her cave and invited special friends (like a dancer, a cab driver, a journalist, a gardener, a painter, and a garbage collector) to explain what their jobs were like. I also hosted a program called "The Low Down on Hi Fi" that gave viewers advice on how to select and install equipment for their home systems.

In 1957, I was in charge of setting up the network television coverage of the House Un-American Activities Committee sessions in San Francisco. The coverage was broadcast by all three network stations. We provided the pool origination facilities.

I was also, coincidentally, one of the unfriendly witnesses that were subpoenaed by the committee. When I was called up, I refused to cooperate on the basis of the First and the Fifth amendments. Cinde and I had many friends in San Francisco, some of whom we knew to be quite left-wing. I was not about to name names of friends. On the stand, I was the first to use the recent Supreme Court decision on the Griswold case, which restricted the scope of such congressional committees. Among the various charges against me was that Paul Robeson was a guest in our home (True), and that Cinde and I signed a "Ban the Bomb" petition (True). And, that I had offered my services to a foreign government (False). I was charged with treason by the committee chairman. I had good support from the community and from KQED. Cinde and I survived. She was my bedrock. Courage is indeed contagious!

In 1962, I had an offer from KETC the PBS station in St Louis. We moved to St Louis and I took over as Director of Operations and Engineering. The technical facilities were pretty well run down. I relished the challenge. Along with the engineering crew we rebuilt most of the plant. With virtually no budget we had to be very inventive. One program I started was "St Louis at 9", a five night a week live remote broadcast program (by microwave) from a different location every night (the first time in television broadcast history). I was made General Manager in 1965. I authored an exhaustive ten-year plan for the future of KETC.

During our time in St Louis we served as one of the "underground railway" stops for youngsters from the "north" who had volunteered to go to the southern states to help register voters – both blacks and whites — who had been disenfranchised. It was a very risky business for the kids. In 1964 three student volunteers (Chaney, Goodman, and Schwerner) were killed by the KKK only a hundred miles south of us. We had to help. We never knew when we would get a phone call from the bus station or some of them would knock at our door requesting a room for the night. Then, after a night's sleep we would feed them and send them off in the morning.

Soon, the Globe Democrat, a hard right-wing newspaper, came out with my "story". For many days on the front page I was accused of being "a communist running our educational station." They pulled out every McCarthy type attack they could. The HUAC hearing, the USMC discharge. The articles were bylined by a Denny Walsh (his roommate was

Pat Buchanan, later to achieve more national prominence). The pressure was immense. Every night, the menacing phone calls came in about 3AM. There was a constant threat of violence. I would check every morning under the hood of my car for explosives.

Throughout all of these travails, Cinde was my pillar of strength and wisdom; my center of gravity. She comforted our children and wiped their tears when they were asked not to visit or play with their school mates. I resigned as president of the PTA.

We decided that St. Louis was not a very friendly place. I began a job search. I went by bus to the national broadcasters' convention in Washington D.C. Almost all of my old friends and associates were ice-cold. It soon became apparent that there was a blacklist. Fear was in the air.

Finally, we escaped to the PBS station in Schenectady, New York, a temporary haven from the black list. They badly needed engineering help and were little interested in my political beliefs. There I — with some very talented engineers — put together one of the best broadcast television studio facilities in upstate NY.

Then on to New York City - my professional "Mecca". In 1967 I joined a television consulting firm and in a couple of years became general manager. We designed the CBS color television studios among many others. I invented and designed Syncrovision, a film/video system, and was assigned a joint patent with ABC. In 1970 I joined the Hubert Wilke Organization, the leading consulting firm in the world in audiovisual, telecommunications, and television. I established the design and professional standards for the company. We had 85 people in five offices (NYC, LA, Brussels, London, and Teheran). I eventually became Executive VP and had charge of some 500 projects in 16 years. Our clients included 45 of the top Fortune 50 companies. I travelled worldwide and designed facilities in some 50 countries.

In January, 1986, I started The Nissen Group, Inc. We were consultants and designers, for both architecture and electronic systems. These typically encompassed television and radio studios, auditoriums and theaters, convention centers, corporate headquarters, schools and universities, etc. My prime specialty was the design of television studios. In the past 50 years I have designed some 200 television studios and have authored several books and hundreds of articles and papers, both technical and social.

During all of our time in Port Washington, Cinde had been intimately involved in theatrical activities. Over the years she was an actress, producer, and director for stage, film, radio, and television. As a theatrical director she had an uncanny ability to extract from her actors the very essence of the play. As an actor she loved getting outside her own personae. She had a bit of Walter Mitty in her, and loved to fancy herself as someone else. We often played private games in this respect. For many years she was an energetic president of The Play Troupe, one of the oldest community theaters in the U.S. All four of our children have been involved in theater and the arts over the years. Two in several Broadway shows. At present they are: a computer graphics specialist and actress (Naomi), a musician and composer (Gregory), an architect, (Timothy) and a television producer/director (Peter).

Cinde took a Master's Degree from Columbia University in English for Speakers of other Languages. We took out a loan to pay for the tuition. She taught English to many foreigners and subsequently paid off the loan from her teaching fees. She reveled in the excitement of her students when they first understood and could speak English.

She and I were left-leaning political activists and were involved in the peace movements during the Korean and Viet Nam "wars". We lived through and survived the shadowy darkness and hell of the McCarthy period of the 1950s. But through it all her interests were many and diverse. She studied and became adept in acoustic design, auto repair, graphic arts, and cooking, among many others. And, she was also a great belly dancer!

Our personal relationship was free and open. From the first days of our marriage we granted each other the freedom to explore, to play, to activate our fantasies without limits. There were no set boundaries other than honesty and openness. The hallmark of our relationship was "total freedom amidst total security". It was that freedom that ensured the greatest devotion to each other. Unmitigated trust was the glue that made this freedom possible. That's a concept that is very difficult for many people to understand. But it was real and it was practiced.

She had a way with words. She was at home, as she put it, in the Wonderful World of Words. When we met she was an editor for the Encyclopedia Americana. She loved to write. And her written words were often poetry in motion. The following is a piece that I am most proud of. I found it in her almost lost archives. Someone had evidently asked her what she believed in. She demurred and said she would think about it. Then, this is what she wrote:

I've been asked what I believe in and what my faith is.

... I believe in only one kind of immortality – that which lives on in the memories of those we touch when alive.

... I believe that tragedies are not caused by wrathful gods nor good fortunes by magnanimous gods.

... I am influenced both by the Shakespeares and the Einsteins and their ability to bring insight into human nature and physical nature.

... I have faith that the sun will come up in the east tomorrow, or if it doesn't, I won't be here to worry about it.

... I believe that the rules of music and the melody of electrons are not that different.

... I have a faith that nothing is unknowable.

... I believe in cause and effect. Things don't happen capriciously.

... I am in awe of the miracle of birth.

... I am astounded by the majesty of the mind.

... I believe that humans can solve problems, especially those they create.

... I have faith in science and poetry and find a great similarity between the two.

... I don't believe in "luck". We make our own luck.

... I believe in speaking up with full voice against injustice.

... I do not believe in a spirit separate from the body.

... I believe that the only permanent thing in the universe is change.

... I believe in my husband, my love, my strength, my comfort, my oneness, my completion, my life.

But to get back to the question that I was asked, what do I believe in and what is my "faith". I assume the question related to religion.

So – Do I believe in or have faith in anything supernatural or paranormal or metaphysical?

My answer is unqualified – not a bit of it.

Cinde Nissen

I wish I could have written that!

Our extended family grew and we reveled in our newly acquired daughters-in-law:

But then, Alzheimers struck.

Rather, it didn't strike. It crept up. By insidious little stages.

I first became aware of Cinde's "memory" problems in 1990. It started with absent-mindedness. As the problems progressed, I began to study the medical literature on dementia and came to the conclusion that it probably was Alzheimers. We both researched the problem together. She was very aware of the diagnosis and when discussing the probable progression of the disease, she said with characteristic courage and determination, "OK, Let's get on with it." From 1991 to 1999 we were heavily involved in nine clinical research programs to study the effect of test medications on dementia patients. None slowed the advancement of this devastating disease. It had indeed become "the long goodbye". I retired from my profession and became a caregiver. Before Cinde was totally incognizant, we frequently appeared on television programs about how to cope with Alzheimers. I felt honored to be in the forefront of the war against this dreadful sickness. As her sole caregiver, I frequently had to remind myself that my loving wife was physically present but mentally absent. In ten years, the progression went all the way from simple forgetfulness, to her not able to recognize who I was.

On January 7, 2002, at 11:31 AM, after almost 51 years of marriage, Cinde took her last breath in my arms. I remember very little of the rest of that day as our children showed up to help.

For the next three weeks my children and I planned a memorial to their mother and to my wife. It was held at the community center theater. I prepared some 200 pictures of her life that were mounted across the very stage that she had performed on many times. They represented her life as a director, a performer, a teacher, a mother, a partner, and a wife. I gave her eulogy. Three hundred people attended and many paid tribute.

For the following weeks, I wrote thank you letters, made phone calls, and tried to adjust to being alone.

And then — a phone call.

It was from "Lilliana" who I remembered seeing at the memorial. It was not the typical condolence call. Something deeply touched me as she related her feelings about Cinde. And she reminded me that Cinde had introduced us when they were both on stage together 23 years before.

Several weeks later, when the haze had cleared, on a whim I phoned her and asked her out to lunch. Our "lunch" lasted over three hours. We were amazed to discover our commonality. She of 33 years of widowed child raising. And myself of 10 years of Alzheimer's care giving. We seemed to fit together like an interlocking jig saw puzzle. We both laughed and shared so much. We stared at each other and she pulled me in with her eyes. It was an instant rebirth for both of us.

Frankly, neither of us can understand how it built so quickly. But I guess the best answer is that both of us had had one hell of a lot of experience. And my grieving was not a recent event but had been going on for ten years. I remembered what a friend of mine once said, "Don't tiptoe into an important project." Or as Steve Allen put it in one of his songs: "Invite her in without a second look".

And now, for the past 12 years, Lilli and I have lived in a committed partnership. She is a gorgeous, sensual, brilliant, loving woman. She is innovative and imaginative. We both enjoy similar activities and are very much alike in so many ways.

Our motto is the Latin phrase, "Hic Et Nunc" (Here and Now).

Yesterday is history.

Tomorrow is a mystery.

There is only today.

A nice mixture of pragmatism, hedonism, and the joy of life.

Lilli and I are forever grateful for the amazing luck that brought the two of us together at a most opportune moment. We move on – but not without remembering the many years of life and love before we met. We both paid our dues and now have the opportunity to enjoy each other in the autumn of our lives.

You might remember the song that starts "For once in my life ..."

I have rewritten it: "For twice in my life ..."

Here's Lilliana's story in her own words.

Lilliana's Story

I am from Ukrainian stock and a child of the 1930's depression.

My grandparents were survivors of the Ukraine steppes in the late 1800s. With the severe economic and political turmoil they escaped the White Russian onslaught by moving to the Austria/Hungarian province of Galicia. There my parents were born. When my mother was 5, the family arrived at Ellis Island in 1905. When my father was 15 he arrived alone in 1907. My mother was 15 when she first married and had a son and a daughter. The marriage ended in divorce. My father married when he was 21 and had three sons. He lost his wife to tuberculosis.

When my mother was waitressing in her parents' restaurant, my father came in quite often and wooed her. They married when she was 27 and he was 35. I was born in 1929, the baby of the family of four brothers and a sister. We shared a cold water flat in the Lower East Side of New York. It had a bathtub in the kitchen, a potbellied stove, an ice box, and a window cold box in the winter. My sister and I shared a day bed in the kitchen. There was a third floor tenant-shared toilet in the outside hallway. My father was a woodcarver and my mother was a seamstress, but during the depression we were on "Home Relief", a precursor of "welfare", along with 200,000 other New York City families.

When I was 10 years old, we moved to a New York City "project". A community center there provided classes in dance, acrobatics, and singing. My mother said I sang and danced before I learned to talk and walk. I was on stage for the first time in elementary school. I remember little about the play except that I experienced, for the first time, the thrill of the applause at the end of the play. I enjoyed sports and a sewing class, which led me to costume design. In my teens I had my eyes set on Hollywood and especially on Errol Flynn whose picture I had on my closet door. But then reality took over. After high school graduation I went to business school to become a "comptometer" operator. A comptometer was a very sophisticated mechanical calculator; an early form of a computer. I worked four years for a firm in Rockefeller Center. While there, I joined the Rockefeller Center Choral Group. In December 1947 we performed in front of the Christmas tree as it was lit.

During WWII three of my brothers were in the service. My future husband Ted also served. When he was discharged from the army, we were married on February 13, 1949. I was 20. He was 22. To help with our income I held a number of jobs. I was employed in the budget department of the United Nations. Eleanor Roosevelt visited our offices occasionally. It was an exciting time for me working with important people from all over the world.

After Ted joined the New York City Police Department we moved to Port Washington in 1958. It was our first house. We raised six children, one daughter and five sons. For some time Ted held three jobs in order to provide for our family. When he had time off we all enjoyed going to the beach, camping, gardening, and cooking. We loved to make yearly trips to visit the farm of Ted's mother in Michigan. The kids learned how to milk cows and enjoyed riding on the farm tractor.

And then Ted died. I was widowed at the age of 40. In the subsequent years I raised all of my children alone with the help of Social Security. Of necessity, I learned how to be strong in adverse times and assert my individuality. I learned how to be a survivor.

One day I was invited by my neighbor to see a play by a singing group called "Port Singers" at the community theater. After seeing the play I realized that I had found something I loved. The next morning I made a telephone call and joined the group. With my love of music, dance, and costume design, I had found a home for my abilities.

Ten years later, Cinde and I met and performed together on stage. We enjoyed each other and laughed as hippies in the play "Sweet Charity". At the cast party, Cinde asked me to join her and her husband Bob at their table. When I saw Bob, I did a double take because he was so good looking. I had met many husbands of friends, but I never reacted that way. Cinde spoke enthusiastically about their life and how she worked closely with Bob in his work. I felt envious, because I did not have that relationship in my life anymore. Some years later Cinde and I were together in another show called "Most Happy Fella". Today, I feel sorry that I never become her friend away from the stage.

Fifteen years later, I heard that Cinde had Alzheimer's and that Bob was her sole caregiver. How badly I felt to learn that this gifted woman was being taken away, and how I admired Bob for taking charge and giving his all to take care of his beautiful wife.

Eight years later, as I was entering the theater for a play rehearsal, I opened the door to the lobby and heard "hello". Looking up, I realized it was Bob. He remembered me. As he came toward me I asked where Cinde was. He said that she had died two days earlier, and that he was at the theater preparing for the memorial service. My reaction was shock and deep sadness. I reached for Bob and hugged him and just said over and over "I'm so sorry".

Something struck me like a thunderbolt. I felt that I wanted to take care of this man. Afterwards I could not stop thinking about him and began behaving like a giddy teenager, causing my friends to wonder what was happening to Lilliana.

Rather than sending a sympathy card to Bob, I got up the nerve to call him and let him know that when he needed to talk, he could call me at any time. I was in his shoes 33 years earlier and understood the emotions he was feeling.

Soon after, we re-met at the memorial service and the reception at his house. I knew little about Bob and realized that I was from a different world than his. But then, as I sat in his house, I saw that he was a family man at heart. I looked out his window and saw his vegetable garden. We ate his homemade chili and drank wine that he had produced. He was the type of man I could feel comfortable with even though I felt butterflies and was at a loss for words when we briefly spoke.

That night when I was home alone, I began reading the story that Bob had prepared for everyone to take from the memorial service. As I read it, I began to see many similarities between Cinde and me. We both loved the theater and community activities. Separately, we had taken adult education classes in auto mechanics, and even belly dance classes. Then I also read that we shared our wedding anniversaries just one day apart.

I decided to call Bob on their anniversary, to see if he needed to talk to someone on this important day in his life. Bob was still living in a haze and dealing with the inevitable activities required after the loss of a loved one. After we ended the call, I said to myself "I'll call him again in a couple of months and give him time to mourn."

Three weeks later, Bob called me and invited me to have lunch. That was the beginning of the rest of our lives. It was a wonderland of discovery when we found how compatible we were.

Today we take care of each other and ourselves. We both enjoy giving and receiving love. We are so fortunate to have found a committed love for a second time in our lives. We have experienced life as adults through thick and thin, but now we both feel like teenagers.

And now, we celebrate thirteen years together.

Both of our lives might be illustrated by the following:

Just in time, I found you just in time.
Before you came my time was running low.
I was lost, the losing dice were tossed,
My bridges all were crossed, nowhere to go.
Now you're here and now I know just where I'm going,
No more doubt or fear, I found my way.
For love came just in time.
You found me just in time.
And changed my lonely life that lovely day.

[Music by Jule Styne. Lyrics by Adolph Green and Betty Comden]

THE SECRET TO BOB AND CINDE'S MARRIAGE?

THE POWER OF CREATIVITY

"It was a warm summer day in 1950...She came across the avenue... By the end of that week we were both open-eyed at what we had created."

Yes, indeed, they had begun to create a whirl-wind romantic relationship that would last 51 years. Both of them had been blessed with unusual creativity from the very beginning of their respective childhoods. And creativity was to become the bond, the glue that would cement their love.

Bob's ancestors came to Kansas in covered wagons. On the farm Bob had learned how to ride horses and bring the cattle in from the fields, milk the cows and drive the farm tractor. He helped to butcher hogs and calves, feed and attend to the cattle, horses, swine, and sheep, cured hams, sausages, and beef in the smoke house.

In 1950, in Oregon State University, Bob graduated with a degree in Science and a major in Physics, minor in Philosophy, all the time being involved in theater, music, and radio plays. In his spare time, he took flying lessons, got his pilot's license, built racing cars and raced on both tracks and drag strips. After college, he went to the School of Radio Technique to study announcing. Soon thereafter, he decided to pursue post graduate work at the University of Bombay, via Morocco, Tunisia, Spain, Egypt, Jeddah, Djibouti, Pakistan, Ceylon, Delhi, Kashmir, Madras, Calcutta and finally, Bombay.

Back to the United States, he put his creative talents into developing, as technical director, a number of television "firsts": the first live TV program from an in-flight airplane and later from a submerged submarine; the first use of live coast-to-coast television via microwave for the Japanese Peace Conference in 1951; The Home Show with Arlene Francis, Hugh Downs, and Barbara Walters; the first live side-by-side pictures from the Golden Gate

Bridge and New York Times Square…and the first color camera crew on the west coast!

Meanwhile Henrietta Schlossberg had been born in the outback swamps of Alabama in 1924, the youngest in the family with four brothers. Her parents had escaped the pogroms of Czarist Russia. When they arrived through Ellis Island in 1906 to move into a little shack overlooking a river, her parents did their best to survive in a strongly anti-Semitic climate. Her mother tried a number of small businesses, selling clothing and pots and pans and her father was a milkman.

When Henrietta started public school, she began to blossom and her creativity came to the forefront. By the age of 10, she had the lead role in a radio play on the local NBC station. Latin and English, acting, piano, harp. In college, she was elected president of the student body and graduated with honors. After college she got a prestigious job as Research Editor for the Encyclopedia Americana. One of the first things Bob and (then) Henrietta decided to do just after getting married was to create a new persona and change her name to Cinde, short for Cinderella. Later she pursued a Master's Degree from Columbia, and became adept in acoustic design, auto repair, graphic arts, and cooking. Over the years she was an actress, producer, and director for stage, film, radio, and television, while Bob became an acknowledged authority in his chosen field of television.

During the dark days of the McCarthy era in the 1950's their creativity was sorely tested as they challenged and subsequently defeated the frightful terror of the times.

After Cinde was gone, "creativity" was also the essence of the relationship between Bob and Lilliana. The melding of one who had 33 years of widowed child raising and one who had 10 years of Alzheimer's care giving required a good deal of relational creativity. But they succeeded, and now have a fully committed loving life together.

Bravo!

THE LAST WORD

In every tabloid, every television show, every conversation at the water-cooler there's an ever popular topic, expressed today in terms of "hanging out", or "hooking up". It may be Texting, Sexting, Facebook, Tweeting, Instagram, Skype, Tumbir, or Flickr. These have all become the instant barometers of today's love lives and relationships.

So how does marriage as an institution fit into our brave new world? In the past fifty years, more Americans than ever are either currently unmarried or never married. In the United States, the median duration of a first marriage is now eight years. Today, only five percent of married couples have celebrated their Golden anniversary. Where does that leave those of us who, at some point in our lives, contemplate marital commitment?

The public interest in successful long-term relationships stories is universal and transcends age, gender and sexual preferences. Young adults, embarking for the first time on "serious" relationships, have been exposed on a constant basis to sensationalized media scrutiny of the marital dysfunctions of popular celebrities and are understandably nervous about a real life long term commitment with a partner. Middle age adults, at the age when divorce rates reach a peak, seek solutions to the marital problems they might now be facing. Older adults, who have sailed through the conflicts, enjoy sharing stories, exchanging tips and reminiscing.

No doubt, marriage is not the choice for everyone. Now days, society offers and respects many non-traditional paths to accommodate relationship needs according to individual preferences.

Yet, research shows that married adults seem to have greater physical, emotional, and economic well-being than their unmarried counterparts. Women in healthy marriages are physically healthier and less likely to be victims of domestic violence, sexual assault, or other violent crimes. For their part, men in healthy marriages live longer, are physically and emotionally healthier and have increased employment stability. Communities with higher percentage of couples in healthy marriages have lower domestic violence rates, lower crime statistics, lower teen age pregnancy rates and higher rates of home ownership. And these positive benefits are not limited to the married couple. Their children, those in households with two married parents, differ from children in non-traditional households on measures such as child achievement and scholastic results.

These research findings are so striking that the US government created in 2005 a *Healthy Marriage Initiative* through the Department of Health and Human Services, to establish marriage promotion programs (http://www.acf.hhs.gov/healthymarriage). The mission statement of the *Healthy Marriage Initiative* (HMI) is "to help couples, who have chosen marriage for themselves, gain greater access to marriage education services, on a voluntary basis, where they can acquire the skills and knowledge necessary to form and sustain a healthy marriage."

Well said, but how does the US Government define "Healthy Marriage"?

"There are at least two characteristics that all healthy marriages have in common. First, they are mutually enriching, and second, both spouses have a deep respect for each other. It is a mutually satisfying relationship that is beneficial to the husband, wife and children (if present). It is a relationship that is committed to ongoing growth, the use of effective communication skills and the use of successful conflict management skills."

One concrete proof of a Healthy Marriage is its longevity. And what better way to study longevity then to visit with older married couples who are willing to welcome you and share their life stories?

As a clinical team, a physician specializing in geriatric medicine, and a geriatric social worker with a background in gero-psychiatry, we have had the privilege of witnessing extraordinary love stories every day. We see in our office couples truly honoring the vows they took over a half century ago, stepping up when the time comes to care of one another "in sickness as well as in health".

More often than not, these couples have faced a lifetime of challenges and developed constructive ways of working solutions together. Some battled alcoholism, others were abused, or cheated on; some lost children, others were sterile and struggled with adoption issues. Money was often short and living spaces cramped. Illness was pervasive and age had taken its toll, bringing chronic health conditions.

But all have retained the love in their eyes of their first meeting. That love is as young and fresh today as it had been more than half a century ago.

How do they do it? How can these octogenarians and nonagenarians be as much in love today? We became simply fascinated by these questions which were puzzling us on a daily basis, while we were tending to their medical needs. We had to find out the answers....

With our encouragement, over a three year period, a group of eleven couples, who had connected through our office practice, decided to meet periodically and explore together the reasons for their extensive marital success. Little by little, they developed a level of comfort with each other, such that they could uncover common factors to their long lasting love. Each author committed to writing a chapter, disclosing openly the problems they had encountered during their own life and the solutions they applied. This book, *I Do,* was born.

There has been a remarkable increase in the number of books published in the last five years on Couple and Marital Issues. The vast majority of these books have been written by psychologists, practicing family and marital counseling.

I Do presents the real voices of older couples, who have endured life in the trenches. It proposes the survival strategies that they have personally developed and tested in over a half century of marital commitment. These are their stories and their secrets.

Gisele Wolf-Klein, MD, Barbara Vogel, LMSW

ACKNOWLEDGEMENTS

This book is a tribute to love and long-lasting commitment in today's disposable society. Our hope is that this book will offer a roadmap for future generations on how to negotiate life's challenges as marital partners. We are forever grateful to the couples who accepted to write their stories so that future generations would discover the joys of sharing the journey of life with a loving partner:

- Marion and Norman (66 years)
- Bob and Marge (66 years)
- Gladys and Morton (61 years)
- Marvin and Elise (60 years)
- Rhona and Desmond (59 years)
- Sallie and Sherwood (56 years)
- Harvey and Phyllis (55 years)
- Grace and Leonard (54 years)
- David and Isabel (54 years)
- Terry and Cal (52 years)
- Robert and Cinde (51 years)... and Lilliana! (13 years)